D1328513

Twayne's United States Authors Series

EDITOR OF THIS VOLUME

Kenneth E. Eble

University of Utah

Jean Toomer

TUSAS 389

Jean Toomer

JEAN TOOMER

By BRIAN JOSEPH BENSON
& MABEL MAYLE DILLARD

*North Carolina A & T
State University*

TWAYNE PUBLISHERS

A DIVISION OF G. K. HALL & CO., BOSTON

Published in 1980 by Twayne Publishers,
A Division of G. K. Hall & Co.
All Rights Reserved

Printed on permanent/durable acid-free paper and bound
in the United States of America

First Printing

Library of Congress Cataloging in Publication Data

Benson, Brian Joseph.
Jean Toomer.

(Twayne's United States authors series; TUSAS 389)
Bibliography: p. 141-49
Includes index.
1. Toomer, Jean, 1894-1967—Criticism and interpre-
tation. I. Dillard, Mabel Mayle, joint author.
PS3539.0478Z57   813'.52 [B]   80-16805
ISBN 0-8057-7322-3

For my wife, Rebecca
For my husband, John

Contents

About the Authors

Brian Joseph Benson received the A.B. degree from Guilford College in 1964, the M.A. degree from UNC-G in 1967 and the Ph.D. degree from the University of South Carolina in 1973. He has published in *Studies in Short Fiction, CLA Journal*, contributed to *Richard Wright: The Critical Reception*, edited by John M. Reilly, *A Bibliographic Guide to the Study of Southern Literature*, edited by Louis Rubin et al., and is assisting in the completion of *Richard Wright: An International Bibliography* with Keneth Kinnamon and Michael Fabre. He is director of Graduate Studies in English at A & T State University and professor of English.

Mabel Mayle Dillard received the B.S. degree from Ohio University in 1938, the M.A. in 1945, and the Ph.D. degree from Ohio University in 1967. She did postdoctoral work in France as an NDEA scholar. She has also published material about Jean Toomer and is presently professor of English at A & T State University.

Preface

Jean Toomer was a gifted and enigmatic literary figure who reached prominence during the early 1920s. His literary reputation has been based on one work, *Cane*, which was first published in 1923. After this date, and during the height of the Harlem Renaissance, Toomer was considered one of the most promising young authors of the era who had found new ways to treat the materials of the Southland and its growing urbanization. The fact that Toomer was black also had a great influence on his growing reputation. Most black novelists were stereotyped as writers obsessed with sex and race problems, employing a stale idiom not conducive to quality material. Probably the single most important contribution of *Cane* was its idiom. Robert A. Bone, in his study of *The Negro Novel in America*, stated that Toomer was the only black writer of the 1920s who competed successfully with Gertrude Stein, Ernest Hemingway, Ezra Pound, and T. S. Eliot when each experimented successfully with the creation of the modern idiom.

Jean Toomer never achieved the critical and artistic promise so many had predicted for him. After *Cane*, Toomer moved away from strictly racial themes. Instead, he continued to experiment with language, style, and theme, moving steadily away from the stereotyped image of the black author. Toomer wrote poetry, drama, short stories, and essays. In fact, he experimented with the whole realm of literature and its diversities. In doing so, he began to alienate his peers, particularly those who wished to capitalize on his enormous talents. Some of these literary productions remain significant. Certainly "Mr. Costyve Duditch" and "Winter on Earth," both short stories, have significance for the modern reader. His essays, "The Flavor of Man" in particular, contain astute and relevant insights.

The purpose of this study is to generally discuss the life of Jean Toomer, comment on *Cane* and its significance, briefly discuss several uncollected selections published after *Cane*, and to conclude with a summary of Jean Toomer's relevance to American literature. Prior to 1970, very little was known about Jean Toomer's personal life and, even now, much needs to be learned about him. Darwin Turner's introduction to the paperback edition of *Cane* contains the most comprehensive summary prior to this study but it is, of necessity, limited. No biography of Toomer has been published. Little scholarly effort has been made to collect his works, to evaluate them more carefully, and to bring them to attention for further study.

It should be noted that only representative works after *Cane* are discussed in chapters 3 and 4. Toomer's poems number in the hundreds, but study of such a large body of work is beyond the scope of this book. Moreover, Toomer was a prolific belle letterist, essayist, and gathered enormous amounts of material for his autobiography, *Earth-Being. Essentials*, a collection of aphorisms completed around 1930, provides a look at Toomer's facility with language and the depth of his insight. Other important unpublished material exists and remains neglected. Rather than discuss obscure and often unavailable materials written by Toomer, we have chosen to limit our comments to those works which are more readily available to the general reader. We have attempted to adhere to the typographical conventions of the original 1923 editions. No uniform text exists and no close textual analysis has been made. Any deviation of quotes from the 1923 edition should be considered accidental unless otherwise noted.

The discussion of *Cane* stresses Toomer's use of language in treating material about blacks. Attentions focused on the structure of *Cane*, which presents a thematic cycle of blacks' adjustment to the pressure of life in America, particularly where they have been influenced by the mores of white society. *Cane* remains a classic of American literature, and even if it were his only contribution, the stature of Jean Toomer would be secure.

This study would not have been possible without the cooperation of Jean Toomer's widow, Marjorie Content Toomer, who resides in Pennsylvania. After Toomer's death in 1967, Mrs. Toomer donated enormous tracts of material written by Jean Toomer to the Fisk University Library in Nashville, Tennessee. She has demonstrated patience, understanding, and sympathy far beyond the call of mere interest. We gratefully acknowledge the debt owed to her.

We would also like to thank Jessie C. Smith, the librarian at Fisk University, who has devoted countless hours of patient assistance, especially with regard to permissions and a reasonably accurate dating of Toomer material acquired by the Fisk University Library. Boni and Liveright, the original publishers of *Cane*, were most generous in granting permission to quote from *Cane*. We are grateful for their contribution to this study.

Dr. Jimmie L. Williams, chairman of the English Department at A & T State University, Greensboro, North Carolina, was most co-operative and understanding during the process of completing our book. Dr. John S. Price, Jr. was of great assistance with the Toomer selected bibliography and offered encouragement, as did Dr. Robert Levine.

Finally, we acknowledge the editorial assistance from Dr. Kenneth Eble, Ms. Patricia McGreevy, and the staff at Twayne. They were instrumental in polishing some rough material into a more finished product. Dr. Eble and Ms. McGreevy, in particular, demonstrated a professionalism and consideration well beyond our ability to thank them.

BRIAN JOSEPH BENSON
MABEL M. DILLARD

A & T State University
Greensboro, North Carolina

Chronology

1894   Eugene Pinchback Toomer (Jean) born in Washington, D.C., the only child of Nathan, a Southern planter, and Nina Pinchback Toomer, daughter of P. B. S. Pinchback, acting governor of Louisiana during Reconstruction.

1895   Father deserted his mother, and Nina Toomer moved to the home of her parents.

1910   Returned to Washington from New Rochelle, New York, where he had lived for several years with his mother and step-father.

1914   Graduated from Dunbar High School (then M Street High School) in Washington, D.C. Enrolled at the University of Wisconsin, where he studied agriculture. Gave up college after a year and one summer.

1917   Turned down for service in World War I because of an athletic injury.

1918   Enrolled at City College of New York for courses in law.

1920   Beginning of his long friendship with Waldo Frank, whom he met in New York at a party given by Lola Ridge, editor of the American edition of *Broom*.

1921   Taught four months at Georgia Normal and Industrial Institute in Sparta, Georgia, where he conceived *Cane*. His grandfather, P. B. S. Pinchback, died.

1922   Beginning of his friendship with Sherwood Anderson and Gorham Munson. Munson was then editor of *Secession*. "Karintha" appeared in *Broom*, "Fern" in the *Little Review*, "Storm Ending," "Nora," and "Harvest Song" in *Double Dealer*, and "Song of the Son" in *Crisis*.

1923   "Seventh Street" and "Kabnis" appeared in *Broom*, "November Cotton Flower" in *Nomad*, and "Gum" in the *Chapbook*. *Cane* published in October.

1924   Spent the summer at the Gurdjieff Institute for the Harmonious Development of Man at Fontainebleau, France. For several years worked with the Gurdjieff Institute setting up classes in New York, Chicago, and Portage, Wisconsin.

1936 "Blue Meridian" and "Winter on Earth" published.

1937 Two pamphlets published by Mill House Press in Doylestown: "Living is Developing," and "Work Ideas I."

1939 Went to India, where he hoped to learn from some guru of a path to a higher form of consciousness.

1940 Made formal application to join Society of Friends.

1944 The first of his religious articles, "The Other Occasion," appeared in *Friends Intelligencer*. Other articles and poetry published in this periodical over a period of years.

1947 Wrote pamphlet "An Interpretation of Friends' Worship."

1949 Delivered the William Penn Lecture, "The Flavor of Man," at the Arch Street Meeting House in Philadelphia, Pennsylvania.

1950 Health began to fail and Toomer entered into an unproductive period. Later, he was placed in a rest home where he spent his last days.

1967 Died March 30 at Doylestown, Pennsylvania.

CHAPTER 1

Behind the Veil:
Jean Toomer's Progression

E UGENE Pinchback Toomer, who is credited with being one of the most outstanding authors of the black Renaissance, was the grandson of Pinckney Benton Stuart Pinchback, lieutenant governor and acting governor of Louisiana during the reconstruction period. Pinchback had figured prominently as well as controversially in the politics of Louisiana. Twice he was denied a seat in the United States Senate, for reasons not clearly known. Some historians maintain that the election returns were improperly counted, while others contend that his dictatorial policies kept him out of the coveted seats in the Senate.

In Louisiana, he was fearless. In Metairie, the section of New Orleans in which he maintained a home, he commanded the respect of everyone. On one occasion, he stood within his yard and dared the militia to enter. On another occasion he was locked in the restroom of a train so that his rivals could get off the train first and control the voting populace.

After these and other threats on his life and popularity, Pinchback moved his family to Washington, D.C., where he purchased a home in a very fashionable and predominantly white neighborhood. Toomer described the neighborhood as one of affluence and said that the Pinchback home was one of the finest in that vicinity.

After the Pinchback family had moved to Washington, D.C., the beautiful Nina Pinchback, his only daughter, was courted and won by Nathan Toomer, a reputedly wealthy planter from Georgia. Toomer says that his mother had a beautiful olive complexion and that his father resembled an Englishman who had spent several years in the tropics. Other than that, he did not classify his parents as to race. Before long, the couple married over the objections of the commanding Pinchback, and Toomer established Nina in an elegant home. But it then developed that Nathan Toomer had run short of funds and he was forced to go back to Georgia. His letters grew less and less frequent and he never returned. Nina Toomer, pregnant and despairing of ever seeing Toomer again, returned to her father's home, where in 1894 Eugene Pinchback Toomer (who later changed his name to Nathan Jean Toomer) was born. As a child, however, he was most often called Eugene Pinchback.

Toomer, in one of his autobiographies, says that he associated with white as well as black friends, yet he attended segregated schools as long as he lived in Washington, D.C. On one occasion, however, he had entered a predominantly white world when his mother remarried and moved to New Rochelle, New York. Dissatisfied because he disliked his stepfather extremely, he returned to his grandfather's home in Washington.

Here Toomer found an ally in his uncle Bismarck, who had a habit of reading late at night. The elder Pinchback regretted that a son of his should spent so much in bed reading. Bismarck would pile up in bed surrounded by books of all kinds and would, if he could, read until very late. Pinchback used every effort to curtail Bismarck's reading. Toomer, on the other hand, admired the sight of his uncle in bed surrounded by literary materials, which reminded him of Robert Louis Stevenson and other authors who had spent a portion of their lives in bed, and he was inclined to look forward to a career which would let him live in that manner if he were able.

Pinchback did not object to Bismarck's reading; at least he did not do so openly. but he did object to Bismarck's burning the gas lights late at night and would keep a sharp lookout on his son's door, and if he saw a gleam of light he would rap on the door loudly and demand that he extinguish the light.

Bismarck and young Toomer schemed against the domineering old man and both were able to follow their interests in reading. For Bismarck, reading had long been a way of life, but Toomer was just beginning to explore materials of the literary world. He began to take an interest in science, history, mythology, and literature. Toomer claims that his interests were instigated more by Bismarck than by the formal education he had obtained in public school. Reading was a real and necessary solace for Toomer.

But the elder Pinchback, who complained about such a small expenditure as a gas light, provided other luxuries for his family. He was especially indulgent with his daughter, Nina.

About this time, Pinchback had moved from the affluent neighborhood in which he had lived and had settled in what Toomer called a "colored" neighborhood. Here, he says that he experienced racial distinctions, and there were frequently black and white confrontations in the neighborhood. For the first time, according to Toomer, he began to know the life of the blacks, and he again attended an all-black school.

In his unpublished autobiography, *Earth Being*, Jean Toomer stated that he was an unruly student. He claims that he had an instinctive resistance to authority. He resented mishandling and much of his behavior stemmed from his resistance to the teachers. He describes how he threw crayons and erasers in the classroom and rolled inkwells up the aisles against the teacher's desk. His recesses were filled with his stomping and the making of strange voices. He felt that he was due special privileges because of his grandfather's position and influence.

Toomer attended secondary schools in Washington, D.C., graduating from M Street High School, which was later known as Dunbar High School. As a student here, Toomer no doubt read the literature of reconstruction and disfranchisement, which was chiefly historical and which aimed at keeping the black man "in his place"; the literature of the plantation tradition, of which Harriet Beecher Stowe and Paul Laurence Dunbar are probably the best-known writers; the literature of the tragic mulatto, who embodied the most objectionable traits of the white and the black races; and the novel of passing. From his teachers of literature and history, who had doubtlessly been trained in black colleges and who generally composed the upper class of the black professional groups, Toomer would have heard the eulogizing of successful blacks in America.

After his graduation from high school, Toomer enrolled at the University of Wisconsin, where he planned to study agriculture. Here, he became acquainted with literature of a different type, the literature of the white world.

Toomer, who was, as Arna Bontemps says of William Stanley Braithwaite, "just a little bit Negro," had entered the university and he says that he was accepted simply as an American. Indeed, in physical appearance, he was hardly distinguishable from white American students, and Toomer claims that he was easily accepted in the society of the university campus. In one of his autobiographies, he says of his early life at Wisconsin:

And it was then, for the first time, that I formed and formulated my views as to my racial composition and position. Going to Wisconsin, I was again entering the white world; and though I personally had experienced no prejudice or exclusion from the whites or the colored people, I had seen enough to know that America viewed life as if it were divided into white and black. . . . In my body were many bloods, some dark blood, all blended in the five of six or more generations. I was, then either a new type of man or the very oldest. In any case, I was inescapably myself . . . if I achieved a human stature, then just to the degree that I did, I would justify all the blood in me. If I proved worthless, then I would betray all. In my own mind I could not see the dark blood as something quite different and apart. But if people wanted to say this dark blood was Negro blood and if they wanted to call me a Negro—this was up to them. Fourteen years of my life I had lived in the white group, four years I had lived in the colored group. In my experience there had been no main difference between the two. But if people wanted to isolate and fasten on these four years and to say that therefore I was colored, this too was up to them . . . I determined what I would do. To my real friends of both groups, I would at the right time, voluntarily define my position. As for people at large, naturally I would go my way and say nothing unless the question was raised.[1]

At the University of Wisconsin, he came under the influence of outstanding professors who, he says, guided his reading habits.[2] Upon the advice of Professor Wooley, Toomer had become acquainted with the *Nation*, the *New Republic*, and the *Manchester Guardian*, journals of which he had never before heard. He became a lover of literature and longed to translate his own experience into works of art.[3]

Next Toomer enrolled in the Massachusetts College of Agriculture and then in the American College of Physical Training in Chicago. The latter school gave him the background for "Bona and Paul." Later Toomer held several temporary positions—athletic director, Ford car salesman, grocery clerk, and theater manager—but his innate taste for life was satisfied reciting poetry and lecturing on subjects varying from dietetics to literature, mainly about Victor Hugo, George Bernard Shaw, and Walt Whitman, all the while writing.[4] During this time, while he was forming his theory of literature as art, he says of himself in an unpublished autobiography:

At all possible times I was either writing or reading. I read all of Waldo Frank, most of Dostoevsky, much of Tolstoy, Flaubert, Baudelaire, Sinclair Lewis, Dreiser, most all of the American poets, Coleridge, Blake, Pater—in fine, a good portion of the modern writers of all western countries. In addition—Freud, and the psychoanalysts, and a miscellany of scientific and philosophic works. And I began reading these magazines: *The Dial, Poetry, The Liberator, The Nation* and the *New Republic*, etc.

In my writing, I was working, at various times, on all the main forms. Essays, articles, poems, short stories, reviews, and a long piece somewhere between a novel and a play. Before I had even so much as glimpsed the possibility of writing *Cane*, I had written a trunk full of manuscripts. The phrase "trunk full" is often used loosely. I mean it literally and exactly. But what difficulties I had! I had in me so much experience so twisted up that not a thing would come out until by sheer force I dragged it forth. Only now and then did I experience spontaneous writing. Most of it was will and sweat. And nothing satisfied me. Not a thing had I done which I thought merited publication—or even sending to a magazine. I wrote and wrote and put each thing aside, regarding it as simply one of the experiences of my apprenticeship. Often I would be depressed and almost desperate over the written thing. But, on the other hand, I became more and more convinced that I had the real stuff in me. And, the "feeling" of my medium, a sense of form, of words, of sentences, of rhythms, cadences, and rhythmic patterns. And then, after several years' work, suddenly, it was as if a door opened and I knew without doubt that I was *inside. I knew* literature. And *what* was my joy![5]

Confident of his ability to become a writer, Toomer left his home in Washington, D.C. to go to New York, where he was introduced to literary society by Lola Ridge, who was then on the editorial staff of *Broom*. Miss Ridge was one of the first persons to indicate to Toomer that his work had merit. In an early letter to him, she said that his work would be talked about and studied twenty years hence. In addition, Miss Ridge added, she had listed his name to appear in an advance advertisement of the January 1923 edition of *Broom*, as a writer whose work was noted for its beauty and vigor.[6] As a result of his acquaintance with Miss Ridge, Toomer met Waldo Frank who, he says, was the most important single influence in his literary career. Frank and Toomer found a community of interest in literature and a permanent friendship developed between the two of them. Frank, as a Jew, had suffered from the prejudicial patterns of American life and consequently he was able to direct Toomer to publishers who would be unlikely to base their acceptance or rejection of his work on a racial plane. Toomer had learned early that it might be at times wise to conceal his racial identity if he expected his work to be published. For instance, a contemporary of Toomer's, Charles Waddell Chesnutt, whose first work had been published in *Harper's* before it was learned that he was black, had been made well aware of the influence of the public on publishers. Concerning the problem of breaking into print, Chesnutt in 1931 wrote:

> I have lived to see, after twenty years or more, a marked change in the attitude of publishers and the reading public in regard to Negro fiction. The development of Harlem . . . with its businesses and poets, its aspirations and demands for equality—without which any people would merit only contempt—presented a new field for literary exploration which of recent years has been cultivated assiduously.[7]

Toomer, like Chesnutt, was certainly aware that the publication of his work might depend on the tolerance of the editorial boards of small magazines to which he contributed as well as on their reading public. For instance, shortly before his first two short stories, "Fern" and "Karintha," appeared in the *Little Review* and *Broom*, John McClure, editor of *Double Dealer*, a small magazine published at New Orleans, wrote to him:

Dear Jean Toomer:

> We are very glad indeed to receive your letter. And we are glad to learn that you have been interested in *Double Dealer*. It is doubtful if you are as interested in *Double Dealer* as we are in you.
>
> Your account of your descent and life confirms us in the belief that you can . . . become an artist of exception and achievement. We feel a high degree of confidence in your future. The blend of races has produced remarkable literature in the past. It will do so in the future, and the work you showed us three weeks ago seems to all of us not only full of rich promise but of rich fulfillment. It will afford us great pleasure to be able to print something of yours, if you will keep us in mind for a manuscript. The thing for which we are grateful in your case is your accurate conception of literature as an art. You have a firm grasp on the aesthetics of the language, and with your blend of racial strains, should produce unusual and beautiful things. The social problems, the bitter riddle of progress and "construction" has warped the genius of so many men who have Negro blood in their veins, as you say. You see deeper than the superficial . . . of the races. Your work has the elemental, universal human reach.
>
> "Fern" and "Karintha" are excellent, more excellent than the other manuscripts. We would have been glad to print them, but we were frankly afraid. The bigotry and prejudices do permeate our subscription list to a great extent. Also there are the guarantors on whom we depend for support. There would have been hostility which, in all probability, would have sent *Double Dealer* on the rocks. We felt that the existence of the magazine was more

important than any single manuscript. Seldes would be willing to print "Fern" and "Karintha" circulating in the North largely. *The Dial* does not need to fear the sort of hostility which we would have to face. If *The Dial* does not use them, it seems that *Broom* would.

In the meantime, keep us in mind. Don't hold back for fear of endangering *Double Dealer*. I am glad to hear that you know Waldo Frank. You have the capacity to surpass him. I have seen nothing of Frank's so good as "Karintha."

I hope that your reference to a period of sterility was unfounded. I feel sure that it is. You seem to be just getting into your stride.[8]

This very important letter of John McClure's is revealing in several ways. It clearly shows the attitude of literary America toward the publication of work by blacks. In addition, it makes the literary world aware that the general belief, at that time, of many Americans was that any ability evidenced by blacks came from their blend of racial strains. Most important of all, however, is that McClure believed that the work of Toomer was superior to that of Waldo Frank but still feared that publication of his work in *Double Dealer* might endanger the circulation of the magazine. Toomer, with rejection such as this letter indicates, learned early that he would have to play the publishing game from both sides—the white against the black. If he wrote as a black, he would surely be accepted by only a limited audience. He would have to write the type of "hate" or "protest" literature popular with the black reading public if he wanted his material to appeal to them. Furthermore, the only blacks able to buy his works were few in number. In addition, those of superior educational and economic attainment were more eager to read of other blacks who modeled their society after that of the respectable whites than of the segregated society of the black world. Few, if any, blacks wanted to read of the primitive black life, as was later proved to Toomer by the few copies that were sold of *Cane*, despite its having received quite favorable reviews from outstanding literary men in leading periodicals.

Toomer believed that his forte might lie in his facility for seeking out the beauty within the lives of blacks and portraying that beauty, but he was dissatisfied with the forms that most of the work of American authors writing about blacks had taken. His major concern, then, became the problem of subjugating the materials he found within the black race to suitable literary forms. Toomer studied his craft conscientiously. Of his repeated attempts to perfect his craftsmanship during the years of 1920 to 1922, he said:

I again got immersed in the difficulties and problems of learning the craft and art of writing. Literature, and particularly the craftsman's aspect of it, again became my entire world, and I lived in it as never before.

And now again I was reading only literary works. This was the period when I was so strongly influenced, first, by the Americans who were dealing with local materials in a poetic way. Robert Frost's New England poems strongly appealed to me. Sherwood Anderson's "Winesburg, Ohio" opened my eyes to entirely new possibilities. I thought it was one of the finest books I'd ever read. Their insistence on fresh vision and on the perfect clean economical line was just what I had been looking for. I began feeling that I had in my hands the tools for my own creation.

Once during this period I read many books on the matter of race and the race problem in America. Rarely had I encountered the nonsense contained in most of these books. It was evident to me, who had seen both the white and the colored worlds, and both from the inside, that the authors of these writings had little or no experience of the matters they were dealing with. Their pages showed very little more than the strings of words expressive of personal prejudices and preferences. I felt that I should write on this matter. I did write several fragments of essays. And I did a lot of thinking. Among other things, I again worked over my own position, and formulated it with more fullness and exactitude.[9]

During the years following the termination of his formal education, Toomer lived in Washington, D.C., where he could observe the blacks who had migrated there from the South, and in these people and their songs he recognized beauty. He had read Sherwood Anderson's attempts to portray blacks. He was an admirer of Anderson's style, but he knew that Anderson had portrayed with only partial success the emotions and latent beauty within the black race. Roomer felt that the beauty and the "full sense of life" within the black race ought to be expressed as art and he believed that he had the power to excel Anderson's writings about blacks.

Sherwood Anderson, seeing in Toomer a kindred artist at work, wrote to him soon after he had seen one of his first published poems in *Double Dealer*. He told Toomer:

I read your "Nora" in September *Double Dealer* and like it more than I can say. It has a note I have been wanting to hear come from one of your race. More power to your elbow[10]

A later reply to Anderson from Toomer indicates the extent of young Toomer's admiration for Anderson's style. An analysis of Toomer's work will show that Anderson's form and style did influence the younger writer greatly. In December 1922 Toomer wrote to Anderson:

Dear Sherwood Anderson:

I read *Winesburg, Ohio* just before going to Georgia. While living in a cabin, listening to old folk melodies that Negro women sang at sundown, *The Triumph of the Egg* came to me. The beauty and the full sense of life that these books contain are natural elements, like the rain and sunshine, of my own sprouting. My seed was planted in the cane and cotton fields, and in the souls of the black and white people in the small southern town. My seed was planted in myself down there. Roots have grown and strengthened. They have extended out. I sprang up in D.C. *Winesburg, Ohio* and the *Triumph of the Egg* are of my growing. It is hard to think of myself as maturing without them.

There is a golden strength about your art that can come from nothing more than a creative elevation of experience, however bitter or abortive the experience may have been. Your images are clean, glowing, healthy, vibrant: singing on forks of trees, on mellow piles of pine boards. Your acute sense of the separateness of life could easily have led to a lean pessimism in a less abundant soul.

Your Yea! to life is one of the clear fine tones in our melody of harsh discordant sounds. Life is measured by your own glowing, and you find life, you find its possibilities deeply hopeful and beautiful. It seems to me that art in our day, other than in its purely aesthetic phase has a sort of religious function. It is a religion, a spiritualization of the immediate. And ever since I first touched you, I have thought of you in this connection, I let a friend of mine, a young fellow with no literary training but who is sensitive and has had a deep experience of life, read "Out of Nowhere into Nothing" when it first appeared in *The Dial.* After having finished it, he came back to me with face glowing and said, "When any man can write like that, something wonderful is going to happen." I think there is. I think that you touch most people that way. And when my own stuff wins a response from you, I feel like a linking together within me, a deep joy, and an outward flowing.

Yesterday a letter came from John McClure in which he told me of your stopping past the *Double Dealer* office, of your reading the things of mine he had on hand. McClure was the real thing, at the right time. The impetus I received from him and from the *Double Dealer* has been wonderfully helpful to me. December *Double Dealer* has just come. It features "Harvest Song." Good.

Naturally my impulse was to write you when I first received your notes. But at that time I was retyping my stuff, writing three new pieces, and putting *Cane* (my book) together. I felt too dry to write. Now the sap has again started flowing...

Won't you write and tell me more in detail how my stuff strikes you. And at the first opportunity I would certainly like to have a talk with you.[11]

Dear Jean Toomer:

Your work is of special significance to me because it is the first negro work I have seen that strikes me as really negro. That is surely splendid. I wanted so much to find and express myself something clear and beautiful I felt coming up out of your race but in the end gave up. I did not want to write of the negro but out of him. Well, I wasn't sure. The thing I wanted couldn't be truly done.

And then McClure handed me the few things of yours and I saw that there was the thing I had dreamed of beginning.

You are right about McClure. He is the real thing. It gives me joy that the *Double Dealer* and other magazines are bringing you forward.

You speak of a book—are you ready to publish a book and will you have any trouble finding a publisher. I would be so glad to go to bat for you—that is to say go see and talk with any publisher when you wish me to.

Also, if my writing an introduction for you would be of any help, call me. . . .

In London, I met a woman of your race with whom I had some talk and with whom I have had some correspondence but in the end I felt that she was a bit too negro.

I felt something like this—that she was inclined to overestimate everything done by negroes because a negro had done it.

In you, that is to say your work, I have not felt anything of the sort. It is equally an indication of an unusual talent. . .

Anyway, thank God I haven't seen or felt it in anything of yours I've seen and I will be surely too glad if you will let me see any of your other things.[12]

Toomer believed that Anderson had woven certain characteristically black emotional elements into his work, but that Anderson had also failed to estimate the importance of white dominance of blacks in Western civilization. Toomer wanted to pursue his own art beyond that point achieved by Anderson in order that he might "give the Negro to himself," or in other words, to express artistically the black's consciousness:

Dear Sherwood Anderson:

In your work I have felt you reaching for the beauty that the Negro has in him. As you say, you wanted to write not of the Negro but out of him. "Well, I wasn't one. The thing I felt couldn't be truly done." I guess you're right. But this much is certain: an emotional element, a richness from him, from yourself, you have artistically woven into your own material. Notably in "Out of Nowhere Into Nothing." Here your Negro, from the standpoint of superficial reality, of averages of surface plausibility, is unreal. My friends who are interested in the "progress" of the Negro would take violent exception to such a statement as, "By educating himself he had cut himself off from his own people." And from a strictly social point of view, much that they would say would be true enough. But in these people you have evoked an emotion, a sense of beauty that is easily more Negro than almost anything I have seen. And I am glad to admit my own indebtedness to you in this connection.

The Negro's curious position in this western civilization forces him into one or the other of two extremes: either he denies the Negro entirely (as much as he can) and seeks approximation to an Anglo-Saxon (white) ideal, or, as in the case of your London acquaintance, he over-emphasizes what is Negro. Both of these attitudes have in their source a feeling of (a desire not to feel) inferiority. I refer here, of course, to those whose consciousness and condition make them keenly aware of white dominance.. The mass of Negroes, the peasants, like the mass of Russians or Jews or Irish or what not, are too instinctive to be anything but themselves. Here and there one finds a high type Negro who shares this virtue with his more primitive brothers. As you can imagine, the resistance against my stuff is marked, excessive. But I feel that in time, in its social phase, my art will aid in giving the Negro to himself. In this connection, I have thought of a magazine. A magazine, American, but concentrating on the significance, or possible contributions of the Negro to the western world. A magazine that would consciously hoist, and perhaps at first a trifle over-emphasize a Negroid ideal. A magazine that would function organically for what I feel to be the budding of the Negro's consciousness. The need is great. People within the race cannot see it. In fact, they are likely to prove to be directly hostile. But with youth of the race, unguided or misguided as they now are, there is a tragic need. Talent dissipates itself for want of creative channels of expression, and encouragement. My own means are slim, almost nothing. I have had and am still having a hard pull of it . . .

Do you ever come down this way? For Negro life, its varying phases of consciousness and development, there is not a better place. I would be glad to share with you whatever I possess.[13]

Toomer believed that Anderson, and his friend Waldo Frank as well, were not able to create art with Negro materials because their minds still "retained a few inhibiting wraiths" concerning race and color. Toomer felt that he himself had a natural and a real proclivity for knowing wherein lay the beauty of the Negro race. This knowledge, he said, became fully apparent to him after he had read Anderson's work and Frank's *Rehab* and *Dark Mother*. Toomer told Frank in a letter:

Sherwood Anderson has doubtless a very deep and beautiful emotion by way of the Negro. Here and there he has succeeded in expressing this. But he is not satisfied. He wants more. He is hungry for it. I come along. I express it.

It is natural for him to see me in terms of this expression. I see myself that way. But also I see myself expressing myself, expressing *Life*. I expect artists to recognize the circle of expression. When they don't, I'm not disappointed; I simply know that in this respect they are second-rate. That in this respect they differ but little from the mass which must narrow and caricature if it is to grasp the thing at all. Sherwood's notes are very deep and sincere. Hence I attribute his attitude to a natural limitation. This limitation, extended, is noticeable in the bulk of his work. The range of his sensitivity, curiosity, and intelligence is not very wide. One's admiration suffers, but one's personal liking need not be affected by this.

There is one thing about the Negro in America which most thoughtful persons seem to ignore: the Negro is in solution, in the process of solution. As an entity, the race is losing its body, and its soul is approaching a common soul. If one holds his eyes to individuals and sections, race is starkly evident, and racial continuity seems assured. One is even led to believe that the thing we call Negro beauty will always be attributable to a clearly defined physical source. But the fact is, that if anything comes up now, pure Negro, it will be a swan song. Don't let us fool ourselves, brother: the Negro of the folk-song has all but passed away; the Negro of the emotional church is fading. A hundred years from now these Negroes, if they exist at all, will live in art. And I believe that a vague sense of this fact is the driving force behind art movements directed toward him today. (Likewise the Indian.) Americans need these elements. They are passing. Let us grab and hold this solution. But in the end, segregation will either give way or it will kill. Natural preservation does not come from unnatural laws. The supreme fact of mechanical civilization is that you become a part of it, or get sloughed off (under). Negroes have no culture to resist it with (and if they had, their position would be identical to that of the Indians), hence industrialism the more readily transforms them. A few generations from now, the Negro will still be dark, and a portion of his psychology will spring from this fact, but in all else he will be a conformist to the general outlines of American civilization, or of American chaos. In my own stuff, in those pieces that come nearest to the old Negro, to the spirit saturate with folk-song: "Karintha" and "Fern," the dominant emotion is a sadness derived from a sense of fading, from a knowledge of my futility to check solution. There is nothing about these pieces of the buoyant expression of a new race. The folk-songs themselves are of the same order. The deepest of them. "I ain't got long to stay here." Religiously: "I [am going] to cross over into camp ground." Socially: "My position here is transient. I'm going to die or be absorbed."[14]

Toomer was aware that the literature of America had not properly depicted the role which the black had played in American civilization. He emphasized to Waldo Frank that the black was in the process "of solution" and that within a few years he would be dissolved into the culture of America, since he had no culture of his own to cling to. And

Toomer wanted to capture these emotions of the "pure Negro" so that he might create art forms. He recognized that the sudden interest of the Black Renaissance in black literature, art, and music was an important movement, but that no American author had ever caught these emotions of the black. He realized that the literature of America ought to include these materials before the American black had completely conformed to the "general outlines of American civilization and chaos."

But the city of Washington, he told Frank, though it provided him with "crude materials," left him literally starved and he began to feel an urge to know the other areas of America, especially those areas where the black population was more dense as well as more primitive. He and Frank, who was also writing literature about blacks, planned a trip south, to the South that was "unspoiled" by integration, miscegenation, and mechanization, where they might observe blacks more closely. To become acquainted with these blacks, Toomer and Frank decided to go to a Southern area where they might associate with these Americans who lived close to the soil. They went to rural Georgia, where Toomer became superintendent of the Georgia Normal and Industrial Institute in Sparta.

Before he left Washington with Frank, Toomer had told him:

> At whatever town we stay, I'll have to be known as a Negro. First, only because by experiencing white pressure can the venture bear its fullest fruit. Second, because the color of my skin (it is nearly black from the sun) at the present time makes such a course a physical necessity. This, however, will not hinder our intercourse. Should make the exchange more complete, in fact.[15]

This trip to Georgia provided Toomer, and Frank as well, with material that helped the two of them to discover America. In his *The Re-Discovery of America*, Frank has attributed his real knowledge of America to the materials he found while on his trip with Toomer: "Then America came to my weariness: the America of beauty and splendour. . . . The Negro South, where with my friend Jean Toomer I had lived within the veil, drinking the warm life that rises and blows within the cane and the other South, bled white, maimed of limb, palsied of head, the stiff-eyes, lovable childish South of the masters."[16]

Toomer's extensive reading had convinced him that the spirit of the black had not been satisfactorily expressed, an opinion borne out by what he discovered among the blacks of Georgia. Having observed that many blacks were a "diluted" form of race, he made another trip, this time to Harper's Ferry, West Virginia, where he had hoped to obtain other valuable insights into the black race. This trip, however, was a disappointment to him. He told Waldo Frank:

Life here has not the vividity and distinction of that of Middle Georgia. Racial attitudes, on both sides, are ever so much more tolerant, even friendly. Oppression and ugly emotions seem nowhere in evidence. And there are no folk songs. A more strident grip, I guess, is necessary to force them through. But Southern life is surely here. Stringy, ruddy whites, worn; full blooded blacks, and I think I see a strain of Indian blood. Localism somewhat diluted by the influx of transients.[17]

In contrast to the "pseudourbanized" blacks of Washington, D.C., and New York and to the "diluted" blacks that he found in Harper's Ferry, Toomer had found in the rural South the sources that he had long sought for in his artistic expression. In a letter to Lola Ridge, he had observed some time after this trip:

The South needs consciousness and pruning. And the courage to break through the New England to itself. Abundance, there is. But those who are most capable of using it are invariably the most inhibited. This for the whites. More so for the blacks. It would surprise you to see the anemia and timidity (emotional) in folk but a generation or so removed from the Negroes of the folk-songs. Full blooded people to look at who are afraid to hold hands, much less to love.[18]

Toomer believed that the literature of America ought to include the artistic expression of the "truth of the South" before such a time in the future when the "Negro of the folk-song" and of the "emotional church" had died completely away.[19] The trip which Toomer made to Georgia gave him what he had been searching for to fulfill his "growing need for artistic expression." He summarized, in his auto-biography, the results of the trip:

There, for the first time, I really saw the Negro, not as a pseudo-urbanized and vulgarized, a semi-Americanized product, but the Negro peasant, strong with the tang of fields and the soil. It was there that I first heard folk-songs rolling up the valley at twilight, heard then as spontaneous with gold, and tints of an eternal purple. Love? They gave birth to a whole new life.[20]

Toomer hoped that his artistic expression about blacks would set new literary standards for black writers. He already knew that the eonomic and professional struggles of blacks prevented their predilection toward literary endeavors. Moreover, the stigma generally associated with being a black had caused them to deny their heritage, whereas Toomer, whose family had once been what are called "good livers," was eager to delve into the folkways of the black and to relate this heritage to the cultural development of the entire United States. "No picture of a Southern person is complete without its bit of Negro-determined psychology," he told Waldo Frank in commenting on the latter's book, *Our America*.[21] Early in his writing career, he had endeavored to develop his talent for recording the lives of blacks. Sherwood Anderson, for one, had believed that Toomer had great talent for "writing Negro." For several years, then, Toomer had concentrated his efforts solely on developing his art of "writing Negro," that is writing about blacks who had not denied their racial heritage nor sought approximation of Anglo-Saxon ideals.

He wrote to Frank concerning his convictions about his literary intentions:

Within the last two or three years, however, my growing need for artistic expression has pulled me deeper and deeper into the Negro group. And as my powers of receptivity increased, I found myself loving in a way I could never love the other. It has stimulated and fertilized whatever creative talent I may contain within me. The visit to Georgia last fall was the starting point of almost everything of worth that I have done. I heard folk-songs come from the lips of Negro peasants. I saw the rich dusk beauty that I heard many false accounts about, and of which, till then, I was somewhat skeptical. And a deep part of my nature, a part that I had repressed, sprang suddenly into life and responded to them. Now I can conceive of myself as aloof and separated. My point of view has not changed; it has deepened; it has widened. Personally, my life has been tortuous and dispersed. . . . Neither the universities of Wisconsin or New York gave me what I wanted, so I quit them. Just how I finally found my stride in writing, is difficult to lay hold of.[22]

Toomer, after he had lived close to blacks in Georgia for a few months, began to write. His sketches and poems appeared in small literary magazines in rapid succession: "Karintha" and "Kabnis" (the dramatic version) in *Broom*; three poems, "Storm Ending," "Harvest Song," and "Nora," in *Double Dealer*; "Song of the Son" in *Crisis*; and "Fern" in the *Little Review*. Spurred on by the ready acceptance of his work and by editors' requests that he submit materials, as well as by the favorable criticism he had received from critics and authors like Frank, Anderson, and John McClure of *Double Dealer*, Toomer devoted his literary talent to depicting the black of the cane and cotton fields. And with this work, his artistic powers reached their greatest intensity in *Cane*.

Toomer's *Cane* heralded the Black Renaissance in Harlem. This exotic work is generally considered to be the most outstanding work of that period. When this miscellany of short stories, sketches, and poems appeared, Jean Toomer was believed to be one of the most promising young authors in America. Waldo Frank, in his foreward to the book, called him the "harbinger of the South's literary maturity," and noted that he had achieved a special significance because his literary style showed that, as a black, Toomer revealed no sense of persecution in his work. *Cane*, Frank added, evidenced

... the emergence of the South from the obsession put upon its minds by the unending racial crisis—from which writers have made their indirect escape through sentimentalism, exoticism, polemic problem fiction and moral melodrama.[23]

Frank, who believed that *Cane* marked the dawn of "direct and unafraid creation," was not alone in his belief that Toomer was the harbinger of a literary force of whose incalculable future no reader would be in doubt. Alfred Kreymborg believed him to be one of America's most gifted young authors.[24] Edward J. O'Brien, when he compiled his list of the best short stories of 1923 and included Toomer's "Karintha," featured the author as one of the foremost writers of that period.[25]

Sherwood Anderson, Toomer's literary mentor, wrote to him that *Cane* was the first work that had treated the black race well. Anderson, in appraising his own novel *Dark Laughter*, which was meant to create a true picture of what might be called the stereotyped black, felt that his own work fell far short of the magnificent portraits of the young Jean Toomer. After he had seen "Nora," one of Toomer's earlier poems, in *Double Dealer*, Anderson expressed his pleasure at seeing such good work come from a black.[26] Andersonian touches may be seen in *Cane* as well as in some of the unpublished short stories and sketches.

Likewise, Gorham Munson, another litterateur of the 1920's, recognized merit in Toomer's work when he saw his earliest writing. In 1922, after he had seen Toomer's "Karintha" and "Fern," he wrote to Waldo Frank: "Jean Toomer interests me enormously....His Negroid lyricism will eventually show great sensitiveness, and as you once stated, he has wonderful materials."[27] In his article "The Significance of Jean Toomer," which first appeared in *Opportunity* in 1925, he said:

> There can be no question of Jean Toomer's skill as a literary craftsman. A writer who can combine vowels and liquids to form a cadence like "she was as innocently lovely as a November cotton flower" has the subtle command of word-music. And a writer who can break the boundaries of the sentences, interrupt the placement of a fact with a lyrical cry, and yet hold both his fact and his exclamation to a single welded meaning as in the expression: "single room held down to earth . . . O fly away to Jesus . . . by a leaning chimney . . ." is assuredly at home in the language and therefore is assuredly free to experiment and invent. Toomer has found his own speech, now swift and clipped for violent narrative action, now languorous and dragging for specific characterizing purposes, and now lean and sinuous for the exposition of ideas, but always cadenced to accord with an unusually sensitive ear.[28]

Toomer subsequently became an ardent admirer and close friend of Gorham Munson. The two, along with Waldo Frank, had discussed literary theories and had evaluated each other's work. On one occasion, Munson had invited Toomer to his tiny apartment in New York where the two had hoped to work out plans for Toomer's future literary productions. But at the time that Toomer had planned to go to New York, Hart Crane, who had been having problems with his family, was already installed in the tiny home of Munson, and was unable to leave because he could not find employment. Weeks passed, and letters flew back and forth between Munson and Toomer while Crane was trying desperately to stabilize himself. Finally Crane found work in a print shop and Toomer was able to make the visit to Munson's home, where the two discussed Toomer's plan for a projected novel, plans which never materialized. Years later in 1967, just before Toomer's death, the aged Munson appeared on television and bemoaned the fact that Jean Toomer had disappeared from America's literary scene, not knowing that Arna Bontemps had already "found" Toomer, who had finally been placed in a rest home in Doylestown, Pennsylvania.

Robert Littell, in reviewing *Cane* for *New Republic*, believed that the book was "an interesting, occasionally beautiful and often queer book of exploration into old country and new ways of writing."[29] He agreed with other critics that *Cane* was a book of puzzling and profound effects and added that Toomer had accomplished well what he had set out to do. His critical estimates of *Cane* indicated that Toomer, as a literary artist, was in control of his craftsmanship:

Cane does not remotely resemble any of the familiar, superficial views of the South on which we have been brought up. On the contrary, Mr. Toomer's view is unfamiliar and bafflingly subterranean, the vision of a poet far more than the account of things seen by a novelist—lyrical, symbolic, oblique, seldom actual.[30]

And Paul Rosenfeld, one of the editors of the *American Caravan* series, felt that Toomer, though his writing was interspersed with "fragmented moods," "hysterical starts," and "tearing dissonance," had the creative power to bring him "high in the ranks of living American letters."[31] Rosenfeld concluded his chapter in *Men Seen* by saying:

Large as is the heralding which comes through him, Toomer remains as yet much of the artist trying out his colors, the writer experimenting with a style. And still, these movements of prose are genuine and new. Again a creative power has arrived for American literature: for fiction, perhaps for criticism; in any case, for prose. Other writers have tried, with less happiness, to handle the materials of the South. They have had axes to grind; sadisms to exhaust in whipping up passion for the whites; masochisms to release in waking resentment for the blacks. But Toomer comes to unlimber a soul, and give of its dance and music.[32]

Toomer, in his personal life, mingled freely with blacks and then circled out to include all literary artists who shared his interests. For awhile, he associated with the black intellectuals in Harlem during the Black Renaissance: Arna Bontemps, Claude McKay, the painter Aaron Douglas, Langston Hughes, Countee Cullen, Jessie Fauset, and Zora Neale Hurston. These black litterateurs, who were at that time achieving their maturity (during the Black Renaissance), also recognized that Toomer had surpassed most of them in the artistry of his work. But Toomer, realizing that he knew very little about blacks because of the type of environment in which he was reared, recognized the fact that he needed to branch out and learn more about his race. Thus, he sought every opportunity to read and digest materials about blacks, and consequently, one of his poems, "Song of the Son," was published in *Crisis*. Claude Barnett, black editor of the Associated Negro Press, when he first saw the work of Toomer, felt that Toomer could not write as he did unless he was a black, but Barnett's white literary friends would not concede that Toomer's style and the polish of his work were inspired by a black heritage. The prevailing opinion of literary America toward blacks at that time may be seen by the following letter from Claude Barnett to Toomer:

Dear Mr. Toomer:

For sometime we, and by we I mean a group of three friends, the other two of whom are literary men, one colored and one white, have wondered who and what you are. There have been several arguments, the literary men contending that your style and finish are not Negroid, while I, who am but the business manager of news service, felt certain that you were—for how else could you interpret "us" as you do unless you had peeked behind the veil?

We would welcome an opportunity to publish anything which you felt would be suitable for these weekly papers which we serve. Good fiction they have never had. The field is really ripe and I believe much worthwhile effort and literary interest would be stimulated by your appearance in these papers.[33]

To which Toomer promptly replied:

Dear Mr. Barnett:

The arguments you have had with your friends, the different points of view and the consequent contentions, are not at all peculiar to your group. . . . The true and complete answer is one of some complexity, and for this reason perhaps it will not be seen and accepted until after I am dead. The answer involves a realistic and accurate knowledge of racial mixture, of nationality as formed by the interaction of tradition, culture, and environment, of the artistic nature of its relation to the racial or social group, etc. All of which, of course, is too heavy and thick to go into now. Let me state then, simply, that I am the grandson of the late P. B. S. Pinchback. From this fact, it is clear that your contention is sustained. I have "peeped behind the veil." And my deepest impulse to literature (on the side of material) is the direct result of what I saw. In so far as the old folk-songs, syncopated rhythms, the rich sweet taste of dark-skinned life, in so far as these are Negro, I am, body and soul, Negroid. My style, my esthetic, is nothing more nor less than my attempt to fashion my substance into works of art. For it, I am indebted to my inherent gifts, and to the entire body of contemporary literature. I see no reason why my style and finish could not have come from an American with Negro blood in his veins. The pure fact is that they have so come, and hence your friends' contentions are thrown out of court . . .

My aim is to direct the people's sensitivity and perception to the beauty that is at hand, and, if I am particularly fortunate, to stimulate someone to an expression of his immediate life.[34]

Toomer felt that his "flesh and blood and spirit" were struggling to give birth to creation, and he continually hoped that he would be able to create something about blacks that would be "in a small measure beautiful." Black historians were also quick to recognize that Toomer had transcended the ugly and the sordid of black life and that he had created a new idiom for the expression of the beauty of the race.

Among others, W. E. B. DuBois recognized that Toomer had unusual talent. He said of him:

The world of black folk will some day rise and point to Jean Toomer as a writer who first dared to emancipate the colored world from the conventions of sex. It is quite impossible for most Americans to realize how straight-laced and conventional thought is within the Negro world, despite the very unconventional acts of the group. . . . And Jean Toomer is the first of our writers to hurl his pen across the very face of our sex conventionally.[35]

William Stanley Braithwaite, who for several years had edited anthologies of poetry, considered Toomer a true artist, regardless of race. Though critics like Alain Locke, Sherwood Anderson, and Alfred Kreymborg usually singled Toomer out as the finest "of his race," Braithwaite recognized that Toomer's greatness lay in the universality of his art. He said of him:

In Jean Toomer, the author of *Cane*, we come upon the very finest artist of the race, who with all an artist's passion and sympathy for life, its hurts, its sympathies, its desires, its joys, its defeats, and strange yearnings, can write about the Negro without surrender or compromise of the artist's vision. So objective is it, that we feel that it is a mere accident that birth or association has thrown him into contact with the life he has written about. He would write just as well, just as poignantly, just as transmutingly, about the peasants of Russia, or the peasants of Ireland, had experience brought him in touch with their existence. *Cane* is a book of gold and bronze, of dusk and flame, of ecstasy and pain, and Jean Toomer is a bright and morning star of a new day of the race in literature.[36]

It is not to be implied that Jean Toomer was the only nor the first American author who was attempting to advance the black as material for artistic treatment. Other American authors were recognizing that the black, as an integral part of American civilization, should serve as an excellent source for such treatment. But Jean Toomer was the first American of black heritage who recognized the possibility of so treating the black and who treated him with such emotion and such depth. He delved deeply into the black's psyche and tried to express his true feeling. In addition, he showed a more accurate depiction of the black world welling up against the white in such a way that this social mingling had never been treated. J. Saunders Redding remarked in a resumé of the influence on literature written by blacks that the work of Jean Toomer was greatly influenced by Eugene O'Neill, Paul Rosenfeld,

and DuBose Heyward. Redding outlined the two aspects of writing
by blacks at this time: the "arty, self-conscious and experimental"
aspect of Jean Toomer and the other type which he characterized as
"naive and sophisticated, hysterical and placid, frivolous and sober,
free and enslaved."[37] Evidences of the latter type may be seen in such
works as James Weldon Johnson's *God's Trombones* and Claude
McKay's *Banana Bottom*. This type attracted more readers. At the
same time, black material was passing into the hands of writers who
commercialized it. Carl Van Vechten's *Nigger Heaven* is such a work.
During the 1920s, Harlem and its activities had become a fad for
white America, both in its social activities and in literature, music,
and art. Most of the writers of this period just prior to the Depression
were concerned with advertising the gaiety of Harlem life or depicting
its sordidness. That the black author was enthralled with the idea of
delineating every phase of black life is borne out by even a rapid
survey of the literature by black authors of the period preceding this
one. Much of the literature, one critic claimed, hoisted the "sewer to
the people's noses."[38] But Jean Toomer had no desire to perpetuate
the traditions common to black authors: the sensational aspects or
the primitivism.

In regard to the materials he was using for his work, he wrote to
Claude McKay:

From my own point of view, I am naturally and inevitably an American. I
have striven for a spiritual fusion analogous to the fact of racial
intermingling. Without denying a single element within me, with no desire to
subdue, one to the other, I have sought to let them function as complements. I
have tried to let them live in harmony. . . . Just how I came to find my stride in
writing is difficult to lay hold of. It has been pushing through me for the last
four years. For two years now, I have been in solitude here in Washington. I
may be begging hunger to say that I am staking my living on my work. So be
it. The mold is cast, and I cannot turn my back now even if I would.[39]

Thus, Jean Toomer broke away from the traditions of literature
about blacks. Inasmuch as his major concern was with literature as
art, he did not cater to the demands of his reading public by treating
the black as a stereotype. He treated blacks who were full of vitality
and emotion, not the dice-shooting, chicken-stealing blacks, but
those who had genuine poetic feelings. For Toomer to make this
break with the literary traditions in writing about blacks required
stringent demands of his own creative powers as well as of his reading
public. Nevertheless, he looked beyond the usual methods of the

conventional treatment of blacks, delved into the study of psychology and philosophy, and sought thereby to improve his literary style.

Toomer was fortunate in that his writing was being done at the propitious time of the "Negro Renaissance," also sometimes called the "Black Renaissance" or the "New Negro Movement." Black musicians and artists had already begun to attract the attention of Parisians before this new vogue of the culture of the black came to America. Jean Toomer was among the main writers, both black and white, who capitalized on the national passion for black life. He recognized the black race as an excellent source of literary material. Now that the race pride of the black himself had been considerably strengthened because of his popularity abroad, black writers began to write about their race more objectively and more frankly, of the upper as well as of the lower classes. Their wider horizons were giving them more educational opportunities and they were being introduced to literature of quality.

Toomer's great advantage over some of the other writers was his superior intellect. Alain Locke, who was a great admirer of his, once wrote to him:

You certainly write well, which in the last analysis means that you have the capacity to think well. Anybody can feel—or limp or even soar occasionally on a spirit of emotion power, but the real sustaining force is that of thought.[40]

In addition, Toomer mingled freely in both white and black worlds, as he says in his unpublished autobiography. His associates at the University of Wisconsin and in the literary circles of New York were interested in literature as art; the same was not always true of early black writers, for many of them were concerned with presenting the best features of the black race to their reading public.

In New York Toomer sought out the literary men who were interested in writing about "spiritual experiences . . . as they occur in America." His closest acquaintances were men, who like him, were devoted to the craft of writing. In New York, his friends of the Black Renaissance movement promoted his work and several of his pieces appeared in *Crisis*. But Toomer sought out and was sought out by intellectuals of the white world.

He became associated with a group of poets and critics who had come under the influence of the doctrine of Ouspensky, author of *Tertium Organum*. Toomer and his friends Hart Crane, Gorham Munson, and Waldo Frank read Ouspensky's book and for them it became a sort of spiritual or religious guide. The belief of Ouspensky, which these four soon adopted, was that mankind was undergoing a type of spiritual decay as the result of materialism that had gripped the Western world. These four young men, at times in the throes of despair because their writing had not been completely the means of providing them with their physical needs, found solace in the teachings of Ouspensky. Toomer, positive that his greatest asset lay in portraying the beauty of life, was taken in completely by this doctrine. Ouspensky had claimed that the most effective medium for the revelation of spiritual realities was through poetry; and this idea found immediate appeal with Toomer. Toomer, along with the others, believed that poetry ought to encompass a new type of language, and Toomer especially believed that the language and ideas of poetry ought to be necessarily obscure and only hint at partial revelation. His method of partial revelation is readily seen in his poetry and throughout *Cane*.

For about a year, these four writers met often and developed a kindred interest in the artistic expression of literature. Frequently heard in their conversations were such expressions as "the new slope of consciousness," "the superior logic of metaphor," "monumental knowledge," and the "interior rapports of unanisme," the latter of which is the doctrine of the French poet Jules Romains. All four of these men became contributors to a special edition of S4N, a small magazine devoted to the arts, one number of which was dedicated to Waldo Frank.

Ouspensky, who had been a disciple of Georges Gurdjieff, a Russian mystic, fell into the background with the arrival of the latter in the United States in 1926. Toomer became one of Gurdjieff's most ardent workers and submitted to the rigid discipline of the mystic, later carrying his program to Chicago; Portage, Wisconsin; Carmel, California; and finally to Doylestown, Pennsylvania, where at various times he set up groups of classes. At this point, Toomer subjugated his creative energies to his desire to know himself more completely, a goal which he followed until late in his life. He became convinced, as a follower of Gurdjieff, that an artist ought to know himself and that he ought to achieve personal wholeness. Thus, if an artist should come to know himself, he could then control himself and his desires. Gorham Munson, who was also a disciple of the Gurdjieff movement, believed that Toomer was one of the most effective followers and made this comment about him and his literary work as it pertained to his interest in the Gurdjieff movement:

He is a dynamic symbol of what all artists of our time should be doing if they are to command our trust. He has mastered his craft. Now he seeks a purpose that will convince him that his craft is nobly employed. Obviously to his search there is no end, but in his search there is bound to occur a fusion of his experiences, and it is this fused experience that will give profundity to his later work. His way is not the way of the minor art master, but the way of the major master of art. And that is why his potential literary significance outweighs the actualized literary significance of so many of his contemporaries.[41]

Munson, like other critics of Toomer's day, was confident that the young poet-novelist was attaining a new level in his work. Along with Toomer, he too became deeply involved in the Gurdjieff system, but Toomer went one step further than Munson and the others. Beginning in 1924, he spent two summers at the Gurdjieff Institute in Fontainebleau in France, and returned to America intent upon inculcating the Gurdjieff system in the young Harlemites with whom he had been associating. Some of them joined him in his enthusiasm, but most of these young black authors were struggling to earn a livelihood and the Gurdjieff system held little appeal for the moneyless enthusiasts. Gurdjieff required that a participant give up his assets to the group and that he spend his entire time in contemplation and study in order that he might be able to subjugate the will of the body to the consciousness. One of Munson's strongest tributes to Toomer may be seen in the following quotation:

It is plain that he has strong instincts, welling and deep and delicate emotions, and a more discriminating and analytical intellect (more fully revealed in his critical work): and these are all keenly aware of life. This life that floods in upon his psychology Toomer finds to be potent and sweet, colorful and singing, interesting and puzzling, pathetic and worthy of respect; he is able to accept it—perhaps because his survey of it shows it to be beautiful and mysterious. At any rate, the only fully adumbrated attitude in *Cane* is that of the spectatorial artist. But that raises the question: Under what circumstances can the artist be the spectator?[42]

The years following the publication of *Cane* were difficult years for Jean Toomer, quite apart from his involvement with the Gurdjieff movement. He patiently waited for the royalties from *Cane*, but few volumes sold. There were only a few blacks able to purchase *Cane*, and others did not care for its style.

Contrary to the expectation of Toomer's contemporaries, his work did not ascend to a new level. The black life which Toomer had once found to be "potent and sweet" ceased to appeal to him, and he removed himself from black circles. Unfortunately, for a few years after the publication of *Cane* and a few other minor works, the main concern of Toomer seemed to be the Gurdjieff movement. His activities with the work of Gurdjieff took precedence over his literary work. Although he did continue to write, only a handful of pieces were published. In 1925, "Easter," which Gorham Munson says was the best selection that Toomer had ever written, appeared in the *Little Review*. Two years later, "Mr. Costyve Duditch," "White Arrow," and "Reflections" appeared in *Dial*. "York Beach," the first five chapters of a novel, appeared in *New American Caravan*. In some of these works, "York Beach" in particular, echoes of Gurdjieff ideas may be found.

It was probably Toomer's intellect that explains his continuing preoccupation with Gurdjieff and the effect it had on his writing. Engulfed in the Gurdjieff movement, he had a new outlet in order to unify his fragmented self. One of his disciples, Aaron Douglas, the painter, was mildly amusing with his account of Toomer's involvement with the movement in Harlem. Douglas, a Fisk University professor, had read the Toomer manuscripts there and was quite skeptical of some of the details contained in the letters and papers. Douglas was not completely taken by the movement and he left the Harlem Gurdjieff activity to help with the famous paintings adorning the train terminal in Cincinnati.

Toomer was persistent, however. Finding no disciples in Washington, he removed himself to Chicago. There he became the savior for many people. First of all, he gave a series of lectures entitled "The Psychology and Craft of Writing," under the sponsorship of Baker Brownell, Ferdinand Schevill, and Edward Sapir. His audiences were composed of some of the wealthiest and most intellectual of the Chicagoans. Other persons included writers and journalists, among them Zona Gale Breeze, a popular writer of the 1930s. Her protégé, Margery Bodine Latimer, who was to become Toomer's first wife, was also a member. She herself was past-master with writing and publishing. Toomer's lectures were highly successful although it seems that Toomer did little preparation. He spoke without manuscript or notes, yet held his audiences enthralled. From this nucleus sprang the groups that were to make up the famous Portage, Wisconsin, series of Gurdjieff lectures, where Toomer had relocated.

Toomer, in charge of the Gurdjieff lectures, rented an old farmhouse where the initiates met. The Gurdjieff students were expected to give up all of their worldly possessions, so finances were not a problem. Following the group from Chicago where Chauncy and Yvonne DuPee, who were later to be embroiled in a divorce scandal that was covered by newspapers over a wide area of Illinois and the same room and participants were encouraged to sleep as little as possible and to spend a great amount of time in meditation.

Finally, the Gurdjieff group became involved in a public scandal and authorities investigated the unusual living arrangements. Toomer, always ready to defend himself with his engaging personality, soon convinced the reporters that nothing was amiss. Although this group was shortlived, Toomer never lost his interest. The group dissolved when Toomer announced his intentions to marry Margery Bodine Latimer, a wise decision in as much as Miss Latimer had a steady income from the royalties on her books.

Toomer and Margery Latimer were married in October 1931 in an elaborate church ceremony, with Miss Latimer wearing a flowing black wedding gown. The wedding was publicized in local newspapers and Toomer was listed as the author of *Essentials: Definitions and Aphorisms* (1931). No mention was made of his having authored the book *Cane*, a tactic no doubt designed to conceal his racial identity, since he had listed himself as white on the marriage license.

With the marriage of Toomer and Latimer, the Gurdjieff movement began to disintegrate. Some of the participants tried to revitalize the group, but Toomer's electrifying personality was absent. He and Margery soon left for Carmel, California, where they were to spend a very happy year, looking forward to parenthood. This was not the first trip to the Southwest for Toomer, for he had visited New Mexico in 1925 to lecture on Gurdjieff at the request of Mabel Dodge Luhan. So, again Toomer was drifting about in search of a purpose in life, and he found the Southwest a likely place. Some of the writers he met in Carmel were D. H. and Frieda Lawrence, Robinson Jeffers, and Witter Bynner. Toomer's reviews of a D. H. Lawrence book were carried in the *New Mexico Sentinel.*

Armed with his ever-growing manuscripts, Toomer spent an enjoyable winter with other intellectuals. Unfortunately, however, word leaked out that Nathan Jean Toomer (the new name that he had adopted) was the same Jean Toomer who had authored *Cane.* At that time many states forbade the marriage of whites and blacks, but Wisconsin, where he and Margery Latimer had married, did not.

Nevertheless, sensation-hungry reporters from *Time* rushed to California to interview Toomer and to find out if he were really a black. His only answer was that he was of the American race. Margery, in her letters to her parents, deplored the unfortunate news, for articles had appeared in Milwaukee; Portage, Wisconsin; and Chicago papers.

One of Toomer's former Gurdjieff students, the wealthy Yvonne DuPee from Chicago, wrote to him in a letter dated April 4, 1932, soon after the article in *Time* had appeared:

. . . There was certainly plenty in the Milwaukee papers but nothing would have reached Chicago if it had not been for the outrageous article in *Time*. It makes me completely fire to think of it. And what to do about it? That you should be subjected to the whole thing is horrible. The tone of it, the vindictive insolent tone of it, makes me boil. You have been put in a most difficult position. Your plan is of course the best—the magazine article about your position. But I wish that *Time* could be made to retract. They are always apologizing—this is a time when they certainly should. Who should make them is the question—and how. Of course it is widely read and Chicago to some extent will know about *it*. But of course, it will blow over and people will forget it. The world is in a position of such seriousness the proper values are really beginning to emerge a bit. One sees it in most people—more tolerance, more understanding, less smallness—newspapers excepted. You certainly have had lots to spare. But you can survive them and make excellent use of them. It cannot really affect you. But we will all continue to feel very badly for the injustice and wrongness of it.

For heaven's sake, don't publish the book. Don't let anyone persuade you otherwise.

. . . Zona Gale paid no attention to the Portage scandal about Jean Toomer. . . . She said she did not care—she admired and felt most fond of you and everyone.[43]

Soon after the appearance of the article in *Time*, sales of Margery Latimer's books declined. Toomer decided to clear up any doubt about his black ancestry, and had printed a small pamphlet called "A Fact and Some Fictions," which he circulated among his admirers. The text of the entire pamphlet is printed below.

Well, it comes into the half light again, this story, this trumped up ghost. It is dragged out of an unreal past for sport and scare by those who seem to like sport of this kind and believe that it will scare. Very well, then, let us look at this fiction. Let us, however, move it from the half light, where it may seem to have some slight substance, into the light of day.

Speaking for myself, I do not half mind the sport, and I have long since ceased to be troubled by the scare. The ghost can cavort all he wants, all anybody wants, so far as I am concerned. Nevertheless, for the sake of those associated with me now, and those who will be associated with me in the future, some facts, publicly stated, are in order.

The facts, as I know them, are these. As everyone knows, Negroes in the South were enfranchised after the Civil War. My grandfather, P. B. S. Pinchback, was a young man at the time, living in New Orleans or thereabouts, and he had political ambitions. Indeed he seems to have had more than ambition, he seems to have had political talent and no small amount of feeling for his fellow men. Pinchback, according to the kind of hearsay that we usually go on, came of stock predominantly Scotch, Welsh and German. I am not prepared to state as fact that there was, or that there was not, some Negro or Indian blood in the family. I really do not know. However, no other member of his immediate family was, or was regarded as, a Negro. He himself, by looks, color, and features, was evidently white.

Whereas others would have thought it to their disadvantage to claim Negro blood, Pinchback thought it to his advantage. So he claimed it, and advertised the claim. And, as it proved, he was right in thinking this would be to his political advantage. Perhaps, also, it was to his human advantage. It was one of the factors that drew the large Negro vote to him, and drew him to the Negro as a champion of their interests. It was one of the factors that accounted for his rise as the most powerful figure of Louisiana politics of that time.

Thus it happened that he and his family became associated with the Negro. And he, I may add, remained loyal to this association to the end of his life. Thus it happened that there were grounds for associating me, his grandson, with the Negro. With me, however, there is neither reason nor motive for claiming to have Negro blood. So I do not claim it. Others, however, have occasionally seen fit to claim it for me. No harm is done. Perhaps good is done. Negro blood is human blood. I have never subscribed to the false belief that one blood is intrinsically inferior or superior to another. This belief is but prejudice and superstition.

I am I, for better or worse. If Negro blood is among the bloods that make me what I am, then the Negro blood, along with others, shares in producing whatever virtues I may have, and also shares in producing whatever vices I may have. Blood is blood. Human beings are human beings. I am I. Whatever I was born with, I still have. But, be it noted I both have and am some things I was not born with. People, I think, should be chiefly evaluated from the point of view of what they have made of themselves, what they, by human effort, have been able to make of the original equipment. This, it seems to me, is the vital matter, is the human view, is the creative issue. If, then, I have made something of myself as a human being, all my bloods are to be thanked. If, on the contrary, I have sunk down below the level of my inheritance, not my bloods but only I myself am to blame.

In view of the above considerations it will be understood why, on the one hand, I do not give racial factors much weight in my evaluations of human beings, and why, on the other hand, I have neither claimed to have or disclaimed having Negro blood. If I have I have, if I haven't I haven't—and that's that. In either case, I am I and I remain I.

As for being a Negro, this of course I am not—neither biologically nor socially. What I am is or soon becomes evident to those who come in contact with me, the reality. In biological fact I am, as are all Americans, a member of a new people that is forming in this country. If we call this people the Americans, then biologically and racially I am an American. In sociological fact I am also an American. I live as an American, always have and always will, except as I develop beyond the national moulds and become a citizen of the world in the Socratic sense.

As long as I have been conscious of the issues involved, I have never identified myself with any single racial or social group but have always identified myself with our people as a whole. My reason for doing this, not only in idea but also in living reality, will be understood by all who realize that the only hope of mankind is to rise above egotism, extend beyond partisanship, overcome separatisms of all kinds and re-merge the now different and often antagonistic elements into a unified and harmonious whole. In my thought, in my ideals, and in the very life I live from day to day I stand for Mankind United. This perhaps is the largest and most significant single fact of my life.

In my view, and indeed in reality, the black race is a branch of the tree of human life, as is the white race a branch of the same tree, as are the yellow, brown and red races branches of this same tree. I am not concerned with any of these branches, as branches, except to do what I can to help them to overcome "branch-consciousness," to attain "tree-consciousness." I am, however, vitally concerned with all these branches, and all equally, as integral members of the One Great Tree. I would have each and all work together and come to the realization that all are primarily members of the human race. All are Human Beings. This has been my realization for some twenty-five years. All people are my people.

This being the case, it is simply not in me to favor one above the other, or to claim one or disclaim another. Such concerns are for those who are still imprisoned in "branch-consciousness." The quicker they outgrow these limited concerns the better for everybody. Occasionally, however, situations have arisen which, had I allowed them to, would have inducted me into narrow racialisms. There have not been many such situations. The few have invariably been concocted so as to give trouble or so as to produce a sensation. I met them as best I could at the time. For the rest, I lived through them without harm, perhaps without benefit. They were not pleasant, however. Nor were they befitting. My life, I think, deserves respect. All life, I think, deserves respect.

Now once again such a situation is in the making. For myself I say—Let it be made. Let the story be told again. There will, I suppose, be sport for some, scare for some, sensation for some. I do not begrudge these people their fun. Nevertheless, as I said in the beginning, I am concerned to publicly state the facts and my attitude, for the sake of those who are and will be associated with me. For these people, then, I have written this paper. If it serves them the way I intend, nothing more need be said.[44]

There are some doubts as to the authenticity of many contentions in this pamphlet. At one time, Toomer had declared to Claude Barnett of the Associated Negro Press that he was "body and soul" Negroid, and again he declared himself white. Nevertheless, the question of his race seems to have had serious effects upon Toomer's writings and to have contributed to the mysterious aspect of his later personal life.

In the summer of 1932 Jean Toomer and Margery returned to Chicago to await the birth of their child. Meanwhile Toomer hoped to reorganize the Gurdjieff groups and to finance his family by means of the Gurdjieff experiments. Margery was busy with the manuscript of her next book and, at the insistence of her husband, engaged in healthful exercises. But on August 16, 1932, when their daughter was born, Margery Toomer died. The child was named Margery for her mother and became a ward of Max and Shirley Groves, who were friends of Toomer's and who had not been able to have any children of their own.

While Toomer was in Chicago following the death of his wife his main interest was still the Gurdjieff movement. He had a wide following during the previous years but the number within the group fell off. Proof of his literary activities during the 1930s came when certain of his works appeared in print. "Blue Meridian" and "Winter on Earth" were published in 1936. The following year two pamphlets were published in Doylestown, Pennsylvania. This was probably the beginning of Toomer's affiliation with the Friends Society. Occasionally he had been seen in New York, but he did not seek out the old friends of the Harlem Renaissance group. He was, in fact, a very aloof man.

During the 1930s he began to become dejected because of the many rejection slips he had received for his works. As he said, he had literally produced a "trunk full of manuscripts," a fact which is borne out by the materials to be found in the archives of Fisk University in Nashville, Tennessee. He had completed several full-length works: *The Gallonwerps, Lost and Dominant, Values and Fictions, Portage*

Potential, Eight Day World, Talks with Peter, Remember and Return, From Exile into Being, and the remainder of "York Beach." He had also written short stories, plays, literary criticism, poetry, and psychological treatises. None of this work, it seems, appealed to the publishers. Toomer began to suspect that some were being rejected because he had once been labeled as a black. It is possible that this was true, but Toomer adamantly refused to write Negro; he refused to be limited.

On several occasions he tried to have the letters of Margery Latimer Toomer published but was told that there was not enough interest in her materials. His first wife had been very successful with her works and had published *Nellie Bloom, This Is My Body,* and *Guardian Angel.* At the time of her death, another volume had already been accepted by her publishers.

In 1934 Jean Toomer was married a second time, to Marjorie Content, the daughter of Harry Content, a Wall Street banker. A letter from his widow to Mabel Dillard, July 20, 1967, coauthor of this book, fills in many of the details of Toomer's later life:

Doylestown, Pennsylvania
March 11, 1967

I do not know the date of his marriage to Margery Latimer in Portage, Wisconsin, where her parents lived. She was a sort of protegee of Zona Gale (also of Portage), but so many of those people are now dead. Their child, Margery, was born August 16, 1932 in a Chicago hospital, and her mother died a day or two afterward. Her friends, Max and Shirley Grove (also dead) took over the care of the baby, having been unsuccessful in having any of their own children, and she lived with them in Chicago until Jean and I were married September 1, 1934 in Taos, N.M.

He and I met Spring 1934, when Fred Leighton brought him to my house in New York. I had been hearing about him for many years. My former husband, Harold Loeb was in Rome publishing a magazine called "Broom," shortly before or after *Cane* was published (1923) and a friend of mine, Lola Ridge was living in my basement and using it as office for Broom as American editor. She kept telling me of this very talented young man whom she wanted me to meet (JT), but in spite of the fact that I was in and out a great deal, and they were publishing some of his stories, we never ran into each other at that time. Some years later, my friend Georgia O'Keeffe told me of Jean's visit to her and her husband, Alfred Stieglitz, at Lake George, and also said I must meet him!

Shortly after I finally did, Georgia and I went to New Mexico, where we shared a cottage at a little town, Alcalde—Jean joined us there and in

September we were married. We returned to New York with his young daughter, and lived there until moving down here winter of '34. It was a gradual move—weekends—then protracted weekends—until finally here permanently the following spring. (My children were in their 20s.)

One of the big events in his life was his meeting with Mr. Gurdjieff, in N. Y. at which time Mr. G was giving demonstrations of his group's dance movements at the Neighborhood Playhouse. This was temporarily the end of his "creative" writing, as his whole life was centered on furthering the Gurdjieff work. He spent a couple of summers at Fontainebleau—the G. Institute for the Harmonious Development of Man, and thereafter conducted G. groups in Chicago. I believe that is where he met Margery L. After their marriage they drove to the Pacific coast, and returned to Chicago, or Portage.

When I met JT he was somewhat less involved with the G. work. G himself was in Paris, and Jean began writing his own material again (nothing published). He also became very deeply interested in Friends—did a lot of speaking for them, and a pamphlet in '47—An Interpretation of Friends Worship. From time to time he would have "low" periods, and conceived the idea that he *must* get to India, where he hoped to learn from some guru of a path to a higher form of consciousness. I was quite unenthusiastic because of my belief that a war was in the offing, and did not relish being stranded in a strange country, not knowing any of the languages, with a husband who was anything but robust and a 6 year old child, but his insistence that was what he needed to *save his life* forced me to cooperate, and to persuade my father to finance the trip. Five days after our ship landed in Ceylon war started (Aug. or Sept. 1939). We pursued his goal, travelling here and there, under the difficulties of being aliens in a country at war; he did not succeed in finding what he was searching for. When he was ready to leave the Suez was closed, no ships were on schedule, and we finally landed in San Francisco, Feb. 1940, via the Pacific on Italian and Japanese ships. (before Pearl Harbor)

He began to have spells of illness which the M.D.'s could not diagnose (1940) until finally they removed a kidney which had been non-functioning for many years, so they said. From that time on, he became much concerned with his health—vitamins—diet—etc. always the attitude of a "patient." He did no writing. For awhile he became reconnected with Gurdjieff groups in N.Y. (Mr. G. had died) and even started one here. (Some point he went in for "Dianetics"—now called "Scientology.") There is much I could tell you as background, but I become too garrulous, and do not have the facts and dates which you want.[45]

Marjorie Content Toomer had grown children by a previous marriage, yet she served as mother to young Margery Toomer, who later attended the Friends School at Doylestown. In 1940, the

Toomers had made formal application to join the Society of Friends and were accepted. Toomer worked as a clerk in that school, and interesting anecdotes have been told about his mannerisms. He wrote tirelessly, standing at a counter with a pencil in each hand. He seldom revised his work and many of his manuscripts were lengthy volumes. It is known that Toomer composed some of his autobiographies during this period.

It is not apparent how Toomer's application was accepted in the Society of Friends at Doylestown, for it is possible that the society did not accept "colored" or at least found some way to circumvent their being accepted. According to Marion Fuson, the wife of a professor Fisk University, however, the question of accepting blacks did arise at one of the meetings concerning the admission of a black student. A heated discussion arose and someone mentioned that the school already had a black student enrolled. Eyes were focused on Jean Toomer, who parried the question. The matter was dropped, and Margery Toomer completed her studies at the Friends' School.

While associated with the Friends, Toomer published a few articles and pamphlets. In 1944 "The Other Occasion" appeared in *Friends' Intelligencer* and in 1947 "An Interpretation of Friends' Worship." In 1949 he delivered the William Penn Lecture, "The Flavor of Man" (which was printed and distributed), at the Arch Street Meeting House in Philadelphia, Pennsylvania. Most of his later work was didactic, even the short poems that he published in *Friends' Intelligencer.*

The letters of Mrs. Marjorie Content Toomer have served to clear up some of the mystery surrounding Toomer's later years. As may be gleaned from his own letters in the Toomer Collection at the Fisk University Library, Toomer experienced considerable difficulty in securing publishers for his works, but he never ceased writing. Marion Fuson recalled many interesting facts about Toomer's life and it was she who directed Arna Bontemps (also a Black Renaissance writer) to Doylestown, Pennsylvania, where in 1966 he obtained the letters and manuscripts now to be found in the Jean Toomer Collection at Fisk University Library. When Mrs. Fuson revealed to Arna Bontemps that Jean Toomer was writing for the *Friends' Intelligencer*, little was known of the whereabouts of Toomer. Robert Bone had said that he had declared himself white and had disappeared, and inasmuch as scholars had not yet developed a revived interest in *Cane*, little attention was paid to his "disappearance." But Bontemps, himself the author of several books and librarian at Fisk University, felt that the papers of Toomer needed preserving. He was not aware of the great number of manuscripts that Toomer had already completed, nor was he aware of the many stumbling blocks that had been placed in the way of his publication.[46]

The papers of Jean Toomer had been carefully preserved at Fisk University. A letter from Marjorie Content Toomer to Mabel Dillard in 1967 indicates that, though in a nursing home, Jean Toomer was legally competent, and it is possible that he himself sanctioned the donation of his manuscripts to Fisk University.

Toomer's last years were spent primarily in attempts to preserve his health. At one time, according to Marjorie Toomer, he became a teacher of Dianetics. Suffering from severe bouts with insomnia, he resorted to various drugs and alcohol, habits which he continued the remainder of his life. Later he returned to Gurdjieff work, pathetically attempting to revitalize his ailing body. He had devoted his life to working order and harmony into the lives of all mankind, only to see his own dream vision fail. At this point, his aesthetic writing had ceased and his sole literary attempts were entries in his journal. Most of these notes were concerned with the failure of his body to recover. He suffered several bouts with influenza, gastrointestinal upsets, and pneumonia, rendering him unable to do any creative writing. His health continued to deteriorate, and it was finally necessary for him to go into a nursing home. For ten years he was in and out of nursing homes until his death on March 30, 1967.

CHAPTER 2

Lifting the Veil: Cane

CANE, published by Boni and Liveright in 1923, was Toomer's first book-length work. His early poetry, short stories, and sketches had been well received by the literary world and Toomer was considered a promising young author. These early pieces had, as Toomer said, sought to extract the beauty from black life and to direct the people's sensitivity and perception to that beauty. *Cane* is a further attempt to show the beauty in black life in its various stages: the primitive black, the black who had been semiurbanized, and the intellectual black. Structurally, *Cane* assumes a contrapuntal series of short often enigmatic turns. The text itself is divided into three distinct sections: Section One is set in Georgia and includes six stories concerning women and ten short lyric poems related to the substance of the stories. Section Two is set in Washington, D.C., and Chicago. It includes four stories, three vignettes, and five poems. This miscellany counterpoints the rural, more sensual and earthy elements described in Section One. The Third Section is once again set in the South and contains one long story entitled "Kabnis." It is at once the most enigmatic and, with close reading, the most edifying section in the entire volume. "Kabnis" brings the reader full circle since the protagonist was experienced both rural and urban influences prior to his return to the South.

Before proceeding to discussions of these sections and their individual interpretation, it is necessary to note some general problems concerning the discussion of *Cane*. Three such problems come to mind: the literary classification of *Cane*, the compositional order of Section Two, and projections concerning the influence of *Cane*. *Cane* is classified as a novel in libraries, bibliographic studies, and in most reference works. Nevertheless *Cane* fails to meet the standard criteria of the novel form. Critics also disagree widely over the proper classification of *Cane*. Addison Gayle calls it a "collage of fiction, songs, and poetry."[1] It is also portrayed as "a mosaic of poems, short stories, and intense sketches."[2] Bernard Bell indicates that *Cane* is "an intricately structured, incantational book. Divided into three major parts, it progresses from a highly poetic to a heavily dramatic form."[3] In yet another twist, Edward G. Waldron contends that *Cane* is a "novel-poem."[4] It is evident that *Cane* has been classified as a novel for purposes of convenience and uniformity. That it is not a conventional novel is self-evident. Rather it is a work unique in the canon of Afro-American fiction. Not only was Toomer an experimentalist, he was virtually inimitable. The word "novel" used in this study with reference to *Cane* alludes to a generality at best and no word has yet been coined which would properly classify *Cane* as a work of American literature.

It should be noted that Section Two was composed after Sections One and Three. Therefore, the continuity of *Cane* may rest more readily in interpretation than in the large design Toomer felt for the material. Darwin Turner correctly notes that Toomer lengthened *Cane* at the request of his publisher and not without some concern.[5]

With regard to the final problem, if *Cane* were limited to two early editions numbering approximately 1,000 copies, what impact could it have made on the literary figures of the era and the Harlem Renaissance writers in particular? A solution to the puzzle will be presented at length during the course of sections of this study, but it is apparent that *Cane* became one of those classics kept alive by word of mouth and sheer admiration on the part of readership. This is a verifiable statement since, when it came time for those successful figures of the 1920s to write their memoirs, *Cane* is mentioned time after time as one book which stuck in the mind as an inspirational work. One way of ascertaining the inspirational quality of *Cane* is to undertake a close analysis of the text itself. *Cane*'s unique format, structure, language, and personae led to its becoming so influential a work. The first section of *Cane*, which concerns for the most part primitive women, is a series of portraits as observed by the son of a slave who has returned to the soil of his ancestors for a final vision of his slave heritage. In this section Toomer records the lives of six primitives, all of whom have led unusual lives, unusual in that they have not conformed to the mores of the Southern social system for blacks. These tales of "crudest melodrama" are told from the point of view of a narrator who regrets the dying out of the spirit of the song-lit race and who sees the vanishing aspects of black life with nostalgic memories. The poem "Song of the Son" reveals the attitude of the narrator of this section of *Cane*:

> Pour O pour that parting soul in song,
> O pour it in the sawdust glow of night,
> Into the velvet pine-smoke air to-night
> And let the valley carry it along,
> And let the valley carry it along.
>
> O land and soil, red soil and sweet-gum tree,
> So scant of grass, so profligate of pines,
> Now just before an epoch's sun declines
> Thy son, in time, I have returned to thee,
> Thy son, I have in time returned to thee.
>
> In time, for though the sun is setting on
> A song-lit race of slaves, it has not set;
> Though late, O soil, it is not too late yet
> To catch thy plaintive soul, leaving, soon gone,
> Leaving, to catch thy plaintive soul, soon gone.
>
> O Negro slaves, dark purple ripened plums
> Squeezed, and bursting in the pine-wood air,
> Passing, before they stripped the old tree bare
> One plum was saved for me, one seed becomes
>
> An everlasting song, a singing tree,
> Caroling softly souls of slavery,
> What they were, and what they are to me,
> Caroling softly souls of slavery.[6]

Toomer poured his soul into this poem. Here the land of the slave is seen as surrounded by a pungent "sawdust glow of night" and enveloped in "velvet pine" smoke. The beauty of the red soil (a symbol of barren land) and of the sweet-gum tree in the midst of a country that is practically devoid of vegetation is implied in stanza two. Though he is in a land that is far from the noises of civilization, the son who has returned barely "in time" to catch the beauty of the land does not despair.

The land of the slave is here seen as a wasted section with "red" soil, unproductive to the point that the grass is "scant" and the lands abound in nothing but pine trees—a characteristic of poor soil. The setting of the sun, like the soil that has been impoverished, is symbolic of a dying race of slaves.

The power of song of the black race is brought out in the poet's comparison of the black slaves to "purple ripened plums," which are bursting to be expressed. Like the plum that has reached its peak of perfection with purple ripeness, so has the "song-lit" race of slaves achieved its ripeness, or its fullest expression, with songs. In the songs of slaves, he sees a tragic beauty—tragic because the slave race, along with its customs, is slowly dying.

Like a child who has returned to pay its last respects to a dying mother, so the poet returns to the land that has nourished and given him an appreciation for the beauty of the songs of the race. "One seed," he says, "becomes an everlasting song" before the tree has been stripped bare—before modern (and ugly) civilization has stripped the slave race of all its simple joys. Stanza three implies that the soul is leaving the "song-lit" race just as the race is also leaving its soul in the rush to more civilized areas, where the simplicity and beauty of the race will be lost. Toomer sees great beauty in the people who eke out their lives on the red soil of the land and who assuage the pains encountered in their lives by their "souls of slavery" softly caroled. The son of the soil who has returned finds the beauty of the destitute South preserved in its primitive women, all of who live close to the soil and who perpetuate the tradition of the lives of women in "niggertown."

I *"Karintha"*

The first sketch of the primitives in Section One is "Karintha." It is basically a description of the physical development of a prematurely sensual young woman—a development which will lead to tragedy. Karintha carries her beauty "perfect as dusk when the sun goes down." Even as a child, Karintha elicits sexuality to an unusual degree and as she matures effects an aura nearly irresistible to the men in the community. Even the minister is cast under her spell. He forgives her indiscretions by calling her " . . . innocently lovely as a November cotton flower." Karintha is of noble savage vintage, one who darts past a bit of "vivid color, like a blackbird that flashes in the light, whose "running is a whir," and who has the "sound of red dust" in the road. Karintha is unfettered and a true daughter of the soil of the South.

Toomer projects a major theme of *Cane* in this initial story. Karintha, as a free spirit and uncommon beauty, is misunderstood and misused. Her true beauty lies in the spirit not the flesh. Houston Baker correctly states that "men are attracted to the heroine but fail to appreciate what's of value—the spirituality inherent in her dusky beauty."[7] Men indulge themselves in her flesh, gradually fragmenting her spirit in the process. Karintha mates with many men, granting them their wishes and finally gives birth to a child, animal-like, in the forest. She then buries it there. The narrator summarizes her plight, calling her a woman whose soul (and body) is like "a growing thing ripened too soon." The narrator does not consider Karintha a prostitute, as Robert Bone has suggested,[8] nor does he condemn her for her primitivisitic ways. He sees her only as an uncivilized woman who has carried the African mating customs with her, uninhibited by the structures of her new, adopted country. In "Karintha" we feel the implication that the narrator is expressing his nostalgia for a race that is dying away. He ends the story with an ode to Karintha's wanton beauty.

> Her skin is like dusk on the eastern horizon.
> O cant you see it, O cant you see it,
> Her skin is like dusk on the eastern horizon
> . . . When the sun goes down
> Goes down . . .[9]

The analogy to Stephen Crane's *Maggie* is apparent. Karintha develops in a squalid environment. Her parents are dirt poor living in a two room shack. She learns the laws of the survival of the fittest and stones cows, kicks her own dog, fights the other children in the community. It is a stark bare existence and she is separated from anonymity only by her extraordinary beauty. But beauty is not enough to lift her to the level of heroine. Instead she is victimized.

II *"Becky"*

The second of Toomer's gallery of primitive women is Becky, a white woman who has two sons, both mulatto, thus becoming an outcast of the community where she lives. Although Becky is ostracized she is literally cared for by neighbors. They offer prayers, food, and speculation about her future well being. After the second mulatto is born, indicative of the fact that she has not altered her life style, she remains an isolato. Becky dies when her house falls in upon itself, primarily due to neglect and symbolically because it has been built upon the sand. As Karintha is an overwhelming physical presence, Becky is a psychological presence.[10] This method of characterization develops a loose continuity from the initial story to the second.

The story of Becky is related from two perspectives: the first from the point of view of one of her peers, and next by a narrator who has been drawn to her cabin "Ages" after the hollow report which signalled the chimney disintegrating and falling in, crushing her body. Even before her physical death, Becky is considered dead as a productive, desirable person in the community. Thus, her isolation represents a spiritual as well as physical punishment. Both the white and black communities reject Becky. With the first son, sired by a black man, the whites reject Becky and tend to disregard her very existence. They renege on that commitment since she is given staples of life. But, having committed the unpardonable sin of miscegenation, she is condemned to living in an isolated cabin. The whites call the string-necked, fallen-breasted woman a "God-forsaken insane white shameless wench." The blacks call her a "God-forsaken poor white crazy woman." It should be noted that both white and black call Becky God-forsaken and crazy or insane. Since they believe God condemns those who violate the unwritten laws of miscegenation, she must therefore be without faith. If this be the case, why are they drawn to help Becky? Is it out of a sense of Christian charity or fear that some other spiritual power may be present. Toomer sets up a subtle duality here. Becky is not just a crazy, faithless wench. Rather, she symbolizes the unnatural conflict between the laws of God and the laws of man, similar to the chronological laws so pronounced in Herman Melville's noval of miscegenation, *Pierre*. Nevertheless, both whites and blacks contribute to build her a cabin home and to sustain her. There are both white men and black men who help to build her cabin but who do not openly discuss her existence. The South ignores the existence of Becky, but the pine trees, in whispering to Jesus, recognize the mating of men and women—with no regard for color or for man-made marriage bonds —as a natural function.

Though Becky is condemned by men and women alike in the community, there is a spiritual bond that causes all of them, black as well as white, to honor her and to help provide her with the necessities of life. She lives in the community as a ghost, probably the ghost of a spiritual community of love. As the narrator tells his story of Becky, he occasionally interrupts the legend with a poetic phrase, "The pines whisper to Jesus." When he dares to brave the censure of the public and to enter her cabin, Becky's body seems to be buried under the rubble of the cabin which has fallen in "ages" since.

In this sketch, Toomer has caught the beauty of the life of a Southern woman who, like Karintha, mated with many men. Unlike Karintha, however, whose favors were openly sought by men, Becky becomes isolated by the community. We know no more about Becky than what the narrator relates that he has heard from the "white folks' mouths" and "black folks' mouths." We never see her; her life is an undiscussed subject. Mention of her is made only secretively. The final impression we have of her comes when Barlo, the friend of the unnamed narrator, out of fear, drops his Bible on the pile of rubble that has buried Becky. The only sound that breaks the silence is the rustle of the leaves of the Bible which murmur as if in defiance of the scorn that the community has heaped on her.

The short symbolic death of Becky's life is concluded by a tribute to her: "Becky was the white woman who had two Negro sons. She's dead; they've gone away. The pines whisper to Jesus. The Bible flaps its leaves with an aimless rustle on her mound."[11]

III *"Face"*

The poem "Face" which follows the sketch "Becky" is a poetic portrait of a woman somewhat like Becky of the preceding sketch— a woman whose life has been characterized by emotional suffering. This is a relatively simple, impressionistic poem, showing strongly the influence of the Imagists, but one which is loaded with deep feeling. Toomer had studied the Imagists diligently to improve his literary style and the work of these poets is evident in his poetry as well as in his prose. The subject of this poem is a woman who has known intense suffering and who is approaching death. Just as in the prose sketch "Becky," in which we are given no actual description of the woman, so in "Face" we are given only the barest outlines of the features of the subject. That the subject of the poem has suffered deep sorrow may be evidenced by the imagery associated with the hair, the brows, and the eyes. For Toomer, the eyes are frequently the carriers of intense emotions. In the sketch "Fern," for instance, the eyes are the all-important features of the protagonist's physiognomy. So, in "Face," Toomer suggests the deeper pathos that is involved by giving only a partial description of these features. The poem reads:

> Hair—
> silver-gray,
> like streams of stars,
> Brows—
> recurved canoes
> quivered by the ripples blown by pain
> Her eyes—
> mist of tears
> condensing on the flesh below
> And her channeled muscles
> are cluster grapes of sorrow
> purple in the evening sun
> nearly ripe for worms.[12]

The suffering of the woman is symbolized first of all by her hair, which, likened to "streams of stars," reveals the beauty thereof. Toomer integrates the imagery of water in line 3, "like streams of stars," with the continuing image of "canoes" in the following lines—canoes which are "quivered" by the "ripples blown by pain." In the next three lines, the image of water blends into her eyes:

> Her eyes
> mist of tears
> condensing on the flesh below.

Here the water imagery continues with the eyes being likened to mist condensing on the flesh, then flowing down to her breasts ("cluster grapes of sorrow"). Death and disintegration are suggested in the final lines:

> And her channeled muscles
> are cluster grapes of sorrow
> purple in the evening sun
> nearly ripe for worms.

The final impression created by the poem suggests an image of a suffering virgin. Toomer relies on the presentation of a series of impressionistic images which are related so as to create a final impression, in this case, of pathos.

IV *"Carma"*

Carma, the third of Toomer's primitive protagonists of the Georgia scene, is a crude and Amazonic black woman whose unusual strength and size belie her childlike mind and actions. Like Karintha, Carma is uninhibited, yet she lives with the knowledge that her sexual relations with "others" have broken the moral code of the community along Dixie Pike. Carma feels free and uninhibited as she removes herself from the confines of civilization and races up the highway, "riding it easy," and singing her "sad, strong song."

In "Carma," the romantic and the realistic are poetically blended. Toomer opens with a song:

> Wind is in the cane. Come along.
> Cane leaves swaying, rusty with talk.
> Scratching choruses above the guinea's squawk,
> Wind is in the cane. Come along.[13]

Another of his impressionistic poems, these opening lines set the tone for the sketch. Toomer records here the Georgia landscape as he sees it with the attendant memories that it evokes. Into the silence of the "wind . . . in the cane," comes the scratching and squawking of the guinea's cry, creating a harsh dissonance with the calm of the canefield. Likewise Carma, whose fragrance is the "smell of farmyards," clad in overalls, crude and boisterous, bursts onto this Georgia landscape:

> The sun is hammered to a band of gold. Pine needles, like mazda, are brilliantly aglow. No rain has come to take the rustle from the falling sweet-gum leaves. Over in the forest, across the swamp, a sawmill blows its closing whistle. Smoke curls up. Marvelous web spun by the spider sawdust pile. Curls up and spreads itself pine-high above the branch, a single silver band along the eastern valley.[14]

This poetic descriptive passage paints a romantic Georgia landscape and into it Toomer thrusts Carma—the "nigger woman"—driving a Georgia chariot. Carma has the physical carriage of a man. She is as "strong as any man," and she drives the mule-drawn wagon, bumping, groaning, and shaking, over the railroad tracks, down the rod and into the rumble of cloudy red dust, and up the Dixie Pike that "has grown from a goat path in Africa." Toomer's intertwining of realistic description of an over-sexed, masculine woman with a background of romantic description of a sleepy Georgia landscape lends an unusual tension to the short sketch.

"Carma's tale is the crudest melodrama," says the narrator. The tale is a light one, hardly credible. Carma, who expresses her emotions as a strong and virile man might, rides wildly up the pike, voicing her feelings loudly and fully. But when confronted with demands that she curb her natural desires so that her actions might conform to the standards of civilized society, Carma, otherwise uninhibited, waxes emotionally timid and becomes as a little child. Then, throwing off her civilized cloak, she reverts to primitive and animalistic actions. While her husband is away, Carma has had others and is accused by her husband. "No one can blame her for that," interposes the narrator. Rather than deny or openly face these accusations, she cowers, whimpers, and rushes headlong into the canebrake and pretends to shoot herself. Her husband, after discovering her deception, slashes one of her pursuers and is sent to the road gang.

The character study of Carma is fragmented in details. Carma is unrestrained physically, sexually, and emotionally. She is child-like and impulsive as well as animalistic. "Words wormed her strength, and it fizzled out," says the narrator. Carma follows her natural instincts in her singing, in her loving, and in her work, but she waxes emotionally timid when faced with the necessity of curbing her desires to conform to the standards of a society which does not enjoy the freedoms felt among the more primitive folk. The strength of this sketch lies in Toomer's ability to embody the "crudest melodrama" against a background of romantic description intertwined with poetic prose, and from this to create the impression of a realistic drama.

V "Fern"

Fern, or Fernie Mae Rosen, another of Toomer's primitive women, is the product of miscegenation. She has a Jewish father and a black mother. Her features and complexion seem to convey the sorrow of the Jewish race as well as that of the black race. As the narrator describes her to us, the whole Georgia countryside, her whole body, and her face flow into her eyes. Fern's eyes leave the impression that she is easy because men are quickly fooled by the expression of the sorrow within them. Her eyes, too, seem to bind men to her and to force them to want to make and to fulfill promises to her. So attractive is she to men that anyone who comes to town wants to bring his body to her. When she was young, the narrator adds, a few men took her but "got no joy from her." Even though Fern has experienced sexual embraces when young, in her later years men come to regard her as a virgin. When Fern finds that there is no fulfillment in sexual union, she begins to turn men away, even those "in fever." The narrator, too, regards Fern as a virgin, but observes that in small Southern towns virgins are rare, for in the South men and women, and especially black men and women, are made for mating. The narrator approaches Fern and offers his body as she faints in his arms. He, like his predecessors, is forced to leave Fern. Fern becomes a picture on the Georgia horizon as she continues to loll, listless and seemingly lifeless, on her porch, and the face of the whole Georgia countryside and something which the narrator calls God continues to flow into her eyes.

This prose selection, which is approximately a short story, is composed of a series of imagistic portraits. Fern, the protagonist, becomes realistic through the narrator's impressions of her, but she dissolves into a misty impression as she reclines against the landscape along the Dixie Pike. In this sketch, Toomer builds the final image of Fern upon a portrait of her as a passive creature whose face "flows into her eyes," and the whole of her body blends into the Georgia countryside. Toomer writes:

Face flowed into her eyes. Flowed in soft cream foam and plaintive ripplies, in such a way that wherever your glance may momentarily have rested, it immediately thereafter wavered in the direction of her eyes. The soft suggestion of down slightly darkened, like the shadow of a bird's wing might, the creamy brown color of her upper lip. Why, after noticing it, you sought her eyes, I cannot tell you. Her nose was aquiline, Semitic. If you have heard a Jewish cantor sing, if he has touched you and made your sorrow seem trivial compared with his, you will know my feeling when I follow the curves of her profile, like mobile rivers, to their common delta. They were strange eyes. In this, that they sought nothing—that is, nothing that was obvious and tangible and that one could see, and they gave the impression that nothing was to be denied. When a woman seeks, you will have observed, her eyes deny. Fern's eyes desired nothing that you could give her; there was no reason why they should withhold.[15]

Fern, whose life is symbolic of the dying beauty of the black race as it blends with other races, represents for the narrator the nostalgic memories of an epoch that has passed. The reasons that she is attractive to men cannot be fathomed, for she has a mysterious beauty about her that sanctifies her and mystifies her admirers. Her position in the community becomes somewhat sacred and, the narrator says, "She became a virgin." Men bring their bodies to her, says the narrator, but get no joy from her. They are then struck by an attachment to her that transcends all reality. Around her there develops an indefinable mystery. Toomer has mingled the romantic and the realistic, blended these into mysticism and fantasy, and has reproduced an unforgettable portrait—one that might be called a word-painting.

Toomer develops the portrait of Fern until it resembles a blur of landscape and then the narrator enters and destroys the painting with a touch of realistic narration. He says, for instance:

Her body was tortured with something that it could not let out. Like boiling sap it flooded arms and fingers till she shook them as if they burned her. It found her throat, and spattered inarticulately in plaintive, convulsive sounds, mingled with calls to Christ Jesus. And then she sang, brokenly. A Jewish cantor singing with a broken voice. A child's voice, uncertain, or an old man's. Dusk hid her; I could hear only her song. It seemed to me as though she were pounding her head in anguish upon the ground. I rushed to her. She fainted in my arms.[16]

The narrator mediates between the reader and the dramatic action. "I ask you, friend, . . . what thoughts would come to you . . . had you seen her in a quick flash, keen and intuitively, as she sat there on her porch when your train thundered by?"[17] Unable to dispel Fern's suffering, he consequently becomes as helpless as the previous men have. Like other men in Toomer's work, he frequently finds himself incapable of emotional expression and resorts to rhetoric. "Fern" is undoubtedly one of the best examples of Toomer's poetic prose, in which he intermingles imagistic portraits with romantic short dramas.

VI "Esther"

Structurally, "Esther" may be considered a short story, whereas the portraits of some of Toomer's other Georgia protagonists may be called, in traditional terminology, sketches. Therefore, it is the first traditional short story in Cane. The theme of "Esther" centers around Toomer's larger idea of man's instincts having been crushed by modern society. Esther, one of Toomer's "dictie" blacks, suffers sexual repression because she vacillates between being "dictie," as black society would expect her to be, and being sexually expressive by her tendency to conform to the impulses of her heritage.[18] Like Muriel of "Box Seat," Esther is constrained by the dictates of bourgeois society.

In this short story, Toomer has intertwined the realistic and the fantastic. In the background, we see the lower-class white Southerners who stand agape at, and fearful of, the black religious orgies. King Barlo, who is a vagrant peacher as well as an itinerant cotton worker, engages in verse sermons reminiscent of those in James Weldon Johnson's *God's Trombones.* In these sermons, Toomer has incorporated refrains from spiritual slave songs: "They led him to the coast, they led him to the sea, they led him across the ocean an they didnt set him free."[19]

Esther is a girl who could pass but whose identification is with blacks, though she is in appearance almost white. As Robert Bone notes, Toomer's "dictie" blacks, or the near-white blacks, suffer the most because they have been almost assimilated into white civilization.[20] Esther and Fern are both black women who have suffered such repression. Esther is denied by whites and repressed by blacks; her suffering is the result of her not having been assimilated by either the racial group which she resembles physically nor that which she resembles spirtitually and emotionally. Both Esther's looks and the wealth of her father have caused her to be set apart from the black community. Though she is nearer white, she is forced to live in the black world because of her black heritage. She has no interest in either the whites or the blacks. Her repressed emotions find no outlet until she sees King Barlo, a vagrant preacher who periodically goes into trances during his religious warblings. Attracted to Barlo's black shining face, Esther is entranced by his religious antics and she finds that his image has left an indelible impression on her mind. "He became the starting point of the only living patterns her mind was to know," says the narrator.[21]

King Barlo is black-skinned, physically magnificent, and his face shines. Esther is so impressed by his mumblings and his religious frenzy that she can think of nothing else. Barlo attracts the attention of the community during his religious orgy, and whites and blacks alike are drawn to him, the blacks out of religious fear and the whites because of the awesome fear of blacks. Of him, the sheriff says, "Wall, y cant never tell what a nigger like King Barlo might be

up t.["22] Barlo's accounts of the messages sent to him during his visions
affect the whites and blacks differently. The blacks are "in tears,"
but the whites are "touched and curiously awed." For the blacks, he is
a symbol of their father-king in Africa and he assumes the air of an
African king as he says to them in a bellowing voice:

Brothers and sisters, turn your face t th sweet face of the Lord, an fill your
hearts with glory. Open your eyes an see the dawnin of the mornin light.
Open your ears—[23]

At the age of nine, Esther is so taken by the image of Barlo that
she never forgets him. At sixteen, she begins again to dream of Barlo
and, when a black baby is rescued from a fire, she imagines that she
is its mother and has conceived the baby by immaculate conception.
As she frantically loves the baby, the townspeople merely watch her
and leave her alone. At twenty-two, Esther is still apart from the rest
of the town, and the community relegates her to solitude because of
her father's standing and because of her own aloofness. All day
long, she dreams of Barlo, who is for her the black symbol of
masculinity. She thinks in terms of his strength and his vicious ways:
"Best cotton picker in the county, in the state, in the whole world for
that matter. Best man with fists, best man with dice, with a razor."[24]
Barlow has many attributes of the stereotyped black: he is a fist
fighter, a vagrant preacher, and he is a lover of many women. Esther
has the attributes of a Southern belle: she is very white and pale,
blonde, sweet-natured, and accommodating. At twenty-two, however, Esther decides for herself that she loves the vagrant Barlo and
that she will tell him so the next time she sees him. When he returns
five years later, Esther throws off her lethargy and regains new life
and decides to declare her love for him openly. When she goes up to
him and offers herself to him, she is rebuffed and the onlookers say:
"So that's how the dictie niggers does it. . . . Mus give em credit fo
their gall."[25]
Esther's social isolation is brought about by her near-white
position in the community. Because she has been deprived of
associations with whites and because the blacks respect her position,
she allows herself to become a neurotic, living a life of fantasy. The
world of fantasy in which she lives never becomes a reality because
the blacks and King Barlo as well, humiliate and ridicule her for
wanting to be a part of the only world she can ever come to know—
the black world. Esther's position in the community symbolizes that

of blacks in the American social order. They live in a world of fantasy concerning their complete acceptance into either the white or black worlds. In neither one do they completely belong.

Toomer has peopled "Esther" with characters who are faithfully drawn. Contrary to a practice of many black writers who were his contemporaries, Toomer does not glorify Esther because she is near-white, but rather he shows how she clings to many of the primitive traditions of the blacks. A victim of the belief that her near-white complexion has rendered her unapproachable, Esther is classified as "dictie." Esther, however, has lived in fantasy the only life that she knows she will ever live in reality, that of the black. King Barlo represents for her the first tangible approach to reality that she has ever had. Formerly, she had regarded other blacks as people in a world apart from her. Toomer describes her:

Esther sells lard and snuff and flour to vague black faces that drift in her store to ask for them. Her eyes hardly see the people to whom she gives change. Her body is lean and beaten. She rests listlessly against the counter, too weary to sit down.[26]

But with the arrival of Barlo, who is symbolic of her link with her black past, Esther becomes animate. She longs to have "get-up" about her. As soon as she realizes that "purpose is not dead in her," she throws off her bourgeois "dictie" ways and approaches Barlo and offers herself to him. That is, until she makes her first overture to Barlo, throwing off her acquired "dictie" ways, Esther has allowed her life to be regulated by the dictates of the black bourgeois which apes white society. Now she becomes full of life: "As if her veins are full of fired sun bleached southern shanties, a swift heat sweeps them. Dead dreams and a forgotten resolution. . . . Her mind is a pink mesh-bag filled with baby toes."[27]

That Toomer has accurately visualized a small Southern town is evident. He describes a group that gathers to watch Barlo's religious trance:

Folks line the curb-stones. Business men close shop. And Banker Warply parks his care close by. Silently, all await the prophet's voice. The sheriff, a great florid fellow whose leggings never meet around his bulging calves, swears in three deputies. "Wall, y cant never tell what a nigger like King Barlo might be up t." Soda bottles, five fingers full of shine, are passed to those who want them. A couple of stray dogs start a fight. Old Goodlow's cow comes flopping up the street. Barlo, still as an Indian fakir has not moved. The town bell strikes six. The sun slips in behind a heavy mass of horizon cloud. The crowd is hushed and expectant. Barlo's under jaw relaxes, and his lips begin to move.[28]

On the background of this small town in Georgia, in the heart of the black district, he has placed characters who represent both those who adhere to the customs of the "dictie" and those who still retain vestiges of African voodoo customs. King Barlo, for instance, combines what he has learned of the new world religious practices with remnants of an African religious dance:

Barlo looks as though he is struggling to continue. People are hushed. One can hear weevils work. Dusk is falling rapidly, and the customary store lights fail to throw their feeble glow...across the gray Georgia town. Barlow rises to his full height. He is immense. To the people he assumes the outlines of his visioned Africa.[29]

Toomer shows that there are traces of superstitions still prevalent among the primitives of Georgia. Many of Toomer's sketches reveal that he is highly critical of the smugness of the rising middle class among blacks and of those who try to model their actions on those of the whites with whom they have come into contact. Black critics too felt that Toomer had "betrayed" the race because he did not follow the traditional patterns of black writing. He did, however, as is shown by such an accurate portrait of a small Southern town as in "Esther," show that he perceived black life with great insight and tenderness. He gives a realistic portrayal of life within the black race, showing the relationship of the white, the "off-white," and the black societies.

VII *"Blood Burning Moon"*

"Blood Burning Moon," another study of Southern black-white relationships, treats the rivalry that develops between two men, one black and one white, over a bronze beauty. This episode is based on the folk superstition that a full moon in the doorway is an evil omen, presaging disaster. The story opens:

Up from the skeleton stone walls, up from the rotting floor boards and the solid handhewn beams of oak of the pre-war cotton factory, dusk came. Up from dusk the full moon came. Glowing like a fired pine-knot, it illumined the great door and soft showered the Negro shanties aligned along the single street of factory town. The full moon in the great door was an omen. Negro women improvised songs against its spell.[30]

"Blood Burning Moon" is the last selection in Part One of *Cane*. Rightly placed, it is, in many aspects, a summary of themes, characterizations, and images developed in the preceding pages. It is the most intense dramatization of race relations, the most clearly drawn analysis of sexual rivalry, and a collage of violence, sensuality, and bigotry. The central character in "Blood Burning Moon" is Louisa, a black woman limited by her own blindness to the world around her as it really exists. She loves and is in turned loved by two men, one white and one black. Tom Burwell, her black lover, is violent and headstrong. Bob Stone, her white lover, is less a characterization than a caricature. His relationship is more self-directed and selfish. The triangle, as the reader guesses quite readily, will lead to tragedy.

When each man learns of the other's relationship with Louisa, a confrontation becomes inevitable. Tom Burwell threatens to cut Bob Stone. Burwell has already marked two black men, and it is no idle threat. Stone hears his name used in gossip concerning Louisa and her sexual proclivities. More in anger and chagrin than in quest of honor, Bob Stone rushes to factory town, injuring himself along the way by falling in the cane. He confronts Tom Burwell. They engage in ritual combat which immediately is reduced to a knife fight. Burwell cuts Bob Stone's throat, thus sealing his fate. It is one thing for one black to cut another, it is quite another for a black to cut a white, let alone kill him. Aroused to a pitch of frenzy, the whites form a mob, armed with guns and carrying rope and kerosene. Burwell is captured and silently accepts his fate. Toomer's description is brutally realistic. Not only is Burwell murdered, his body is mutilated and burned. Louisa gazes upon the reflection of Tom's burning remains, believing it to be the reflection of the moon. This image constitutes one of the most highly wrought symbolic elements in *Cane*. The moon is actually "blood-burning" since she is witnessing one of the most horrible consequences of racism. Rather than accept the reality of the situation, Louisa retreats into her own blindness to the real world.

"Blood Burning Moon" is based on the folk superstition that the full moon in the doorway is an evil omen, presaging disaster. "The full moon in the great door was an omen. Negro women improvised songs against its spell."[31] The folk superstition leads directly into Toomer's development of the relationship in "Blood Burning Moon." The relationships here are based directly upon folk custom prevalent among the blacks and whites in the South. True to their background of African superstition, blacks close to the soil accept the authenticity of omens. Louisa, and the other blacks as well, accept the ill luck that follows the appearance of evil omens: the yelping and howling of hounds, the barking of dogs, the crowing of a rooster are proof enough that the "blood-burning moon" presages ill luck which no human being can prevent. Tom, for instance, just before the fight over Louisa, is aware of the ominousness of the full moon: "Away from the fight, away from the stove, chill got to him. He shivered. He shuddered when he saw the full moon rising towards the cloud bank."[32] Louisa also accepts the fight between Tom and Bob Stone as a part of the life within her race: "His black balanced, and pulled against the white of Stone, when she thought of them."[33] She accepts their antagonism as a part of the racial relationships of the South, just as she nonchantly accepts Tom's fate at the hands of the lynching party. But Tom and Bob, each sparked to a sexual rivalry that transcends all racial bars, are pitted against each other because they both love the same girl. And Tom Burell refuses to share Louisa with Bob Stone because he resents a white man having an opportunity to make love to a black woman, while Bob Stone considers it the white man's privilege to have sexual relations with any black woman he wants. He thinks:

No nigger had ever been with his girl. Some position for him to be in. Him, Bob Stone, of the old Stone family, in a scrap with a nigger over a nigger girl. In the good old days . . . Ha! Those were the days. His family had lost ground. The clear white of his skin paled, and the flush of his cheeks turned purple. As if to balance this outward change, his mind became consciously a white man's. He passed the house with its huge open hearth which, in the days of slavery, was the plantation cookery. He saw Louisa bent over that hearth. He went in as a master should and took her. Direct, honest, bold. None of that sneaking that he had to go through now. The contrast was repulsive to him. His family had lost ground. Hell no, his family still owned the niggers, practically.[34]

But his analysis can never allow him to understand Louisa's primitive nature.

"Blood Burning Moon" is divided into three sections: the first, from Louisa's point of view; the second, from Tom's point of view; and the third, from Bob's, shifting to Tom's, and finally Louisa's again. This method made for a tightly controlled narration, enabling Toomer to emphasize the distortions of reality each develop. Moreover, it becomes more readily clear to the reader that society (i.e., the Louisas, Toms, Bobs, and those who blindly accept roles and mores) is also guilty of such distortions. It is remarkable that Toomer was able to make his point so clear by emphasizing distortions, especially since he is able to meld these images in the distortion of the source of the reflection Louisa sees on the door.

The major motif of "Blood Burning Moon" is blindness. The town itself is blind to change. The opening scene describes a cotton factory, dead since the Civil War. It is symbolic of the vestiges of racism still prevalent in "factory town." Louisa, who lives in segregated factory town, blindly accepts separate relationships with her black and her white lover. Bob Stone is loosely connected with the cotton factory motif since he is the son of an employee. Despite all of the folk superstition warning Louisa believes she can control fate by inaction, blindly ignoring such dangerous activity. Bob Stone is blind to his own carnal lust, and the immediate danger in which he places himself. Because he is white, Bob blindly believes it is his right to have Louisa and to humiliate Tom Burwell, who would not dare to retaliate. Blindness costs Bob Stone his life as it does Tom Burwell. Burwell is blindly maddened that a white man is using his "woman." The poem

> "Red nigger moon. Sinner!
> Blood burning moon. Sinner!
> Come out that fact'ry door."

concludes each section of the narrative. It also represents in microcosm, the elements of "Blood Burning Moon." It is a primitive plan to superstition. It presages the burning of Tom Burwell, and it harkens back to the factory town element. It is also the omen Louisa must sing to as the narrative ends.

"Blood Burning Moon" completes the circular movement of Part One of *Cane.* Hints of violence, racial disharmony, and the dangers of sexual impropriety come to function as much as they are implied in "Becky," "Karintha," and "Esther" among the selections. Toomer also places several recurring characters in "Blood Burning Moon," relating it to the previous narratives. Toomer includes "Old David Georgia, who brought sugar soup to Becky, and . . . Toomer's comparison of himself to Barlo."[35] In addition, John Stone, Bob's father, is a character from "Becky." He donated material to assist in building her cabin. These elements remind the reader of Toomer's intentions of circularity for this section and "Blood Burning Moon" meets these requirements very well.

These six primitive women of Section One of *Cane* are meant to portray the varying degrees of beauty found within the lives of blacks who live close to the soil. Of these women, Karintha, the most primitive, is the most free and uninhibited in her way of life. She gives her body freely to men—"she smiles, and indulges them when she is in the mood for them." She gives birth, animal like, to a child which "fell out of her womb onto a bed of pine needles in the forest."[36] And at twenty, she "has been married many times," says the narrator, referring to the spiritual bond that she had developed with men. Toomer's belief that the lives of people who live close to the soil are far more beautiful than those of others is evident in this sketch of Karintha. Toomer has said about the life he observed in Georgia: "There one finds soil in the sense that the Russians know it—the soil every art and literature that is to live must be imbedded in."[37] Karintha achieves a fuller sense of life and beauty than any of the other protagonists of Section One of *Cane*. Becky, who also disregards man-made laws of Southern society by mating with both white and black men, lives close to the soil, but her life has been warped by society's rejection of her. Toomer makes it evident, however, that there is a heavenly approval of her way of life when he describes the flapping of the leaves of the Bible over the mound that is assumed to be her burying place. But Becky's sons are too close to the life of the community to disregard its social laws and are consequently often caught up in fights and brawls in an attempt to maintain their personal freedom and integrity.[38] Esther, the protagonist who is near-white, probably suffers more than any of the others because she vacillates between two identities, white and black, and she soon finds herself living a life of fantasy.[39] Carma suffers few restraints and her hysteria is developed as the result of restrictions imposed on her by society.[40] The antagonism that develops between the two men in "Blood Burning Moon" is a rivalry animalistic in nature, a strong sexual urge for a female. Louisa's racial identity has no bearing on the opposition between the two men. The result of the struggle, Tom's death, means that the black has been subjected to the penalty of the Southern society, in America, lynching. And, in a larger sense, the lynching by the community goes back to the old law of "an eye for an eye."[41]

Thus, some of Toomer's more primitive women, such as Karintha and Becky, live rich lives, full of beauty. But as the "song-lit race of slaves" takes on the characteristics and ways of the master race, in appearance and in living, life often becomes sordid and full of inhibitions. For instance, Fernie Mae Rosen, a mulatto who is half-Jewish, and the almost-white Esther both lack the vitality of their more primitive sisters. Carma, too, when faced with the restrictions of civilized racial codes, resorts to a hysteria that reduces her to a childlike state. Thus, the first section of *Cane*, composed of the lives of these six primitive women, bears out in a circular structure the nostalgia that the poet expresses in "Song of the Son."

Toomer had managed to recapture the tenor and fundamental character of his primitives, each a "plaintive soul" which has prematurely passed from existence in the South. Each woman, in time, reignites this racial memory.

Toomer carries the section full circle since in the literal sense, his primitives are direct products of the slave-holding South and each selection is, as one sees, now an "everlasting song" and a constant reminder of the vestiges of that peculiar institution.

VIII *Section Two*

The second section of *Cane* takes us to Washington and to Chicago, city environments which show how man's essential goodness is warped by the restrictions that he finds in life there. in such environments, the primitive is restricted by houses, buildings, social customs, and man-made laws and aspirations. Some of the feminine protagonists of Section Two (as in Section One of *Cane*) are women whose love-life know no bounds. As noted, these women are called prostitutes by Robert Bone in his assessment of Toomer's primitives,[42] but Toomer prefers to think of these as women whose giving of themselves is a natural impulse that disregards man's laws for the legality of marriage or of the social customs which hold that one mates with his own race only, or perhaps we should say, color.

These protagonists of the second part of *Cane* retain some vestiges of their Southern racial roots. They have not fully adjusted their lives to the confines of the city. The barriers of the city have limited their adjustment to natural life impulses, such as singing, lovemaking, creating, and brotherhood. These protagonists live in the city—in Chicago and in Washington—where the black life of the rural South mingles with that of the urban environment. In these black areas, like that near Seventh Street in Washington, the blood suckers of World War I, bootleggers wearing silken shirts and driving zooming Cadillacs, have sucked the life-blood of the soft-skinned blacks who have migrated there. The stale, soggy wood of the city houses has helped to confine these city people to their drug stores, to restaurants, to cabarets, and to shanties, and their confinement here has been the dominant factor that has distorted their lives. But blacks whose roots are still in the South have helped to give the city an air of vitality.

IX *"Seventh Street"*

Toomer describes this Seventh Street in stale, bare prose, threaded with grim realism:

Seventh Street is a bastard of Prohibition and the war. A crude-boned, soft-skinned wedge of nigger life breathing its loafer air, jazz songs, and love, thrusting unconscious rhythms, black reddish blood into the white and whitewashed wood of Washington. Wedges rust in soggy wood . . . Split it! In two! Again! Shred it! . . . the sun. Wedges are brilliant in the sun; ribbons of wet wood dry and blow away. Black reddish blood. Pouring for crude-boned soft-skinned life, who set you flowing? Blood suckers of the war would spin in a frenzy of dizziness if they drank your blood.[43]

X *"Avey"*

"Avey" is the initial urban story on *Cane* and its placement in Section Two of the narrative demonstrates Toomer's insight into his purpose for the section. "Avey" resembles "Fern" in both stylistic and thematic format.[44] It also reverses the characterization in "Karintha." Thus, Toomer begins to develop analogues and echoes from Part One to supplement a continuity of characterization and setting. Toomer obviously intends that urban sterility is a major thematic consideration in "Avey" and the whole of Section Two. But, he also wanted the reader to measure the geographic and psychological distance between the Georgia selections and Northern selections. It is a successful method as "Avey" attests.

"Avey" is narrated in the first person by a professed sympathetic observer who attempts to sort out the puzzle of Avey's life. This method is similar stylistically to that used in "Karintha." In fact, the theme of maturity, stagnation, and finally death in life coincides with the temporal aspects of "Karintha." Moreover, Avey, like Karintha, takes money from men and gives her body in return. Avey also possesses a sensuality and "an unbridled response to life" like Karintha.

"Avey" begins with the narrator describing how he first became attracted to her. He is sitting with a group of his adolescent friends on V Street, waiting for Avey to leave her flat or a flat used to entertain her gentlemen callers. Their conversation consists of sexual innuendo. He admits that "we all talked dirt."[45] Avey finally comes down from the flat, ignores the waiting adolescents, and goes home. As a group, they wonder what will happen to Avey. Perhaps she will marry and settle down to a life of respectability. This seemingly offhanded remark underscores one of Toomer's repeated considerations in *Cane*. Just beneath the surface, each story, and in particular "Avey," there is a morality element. One must conform to society's dictates, largely encumbered by the Christian ethic. These adolescents believe that if Avey does conform to societal dictates and marries, her moral virtues will likewise increase. One must not become an outcast, shunned from salvation and the fruits of the American Dream. Perhaps this stranglehold society has on V Street youth is best evidenced by the narrator's next comments. He goes home picturing himself as married. he will make her respectable and, in turn, gain the golden girl and respect for himself. Not once does it occur to the narrator that his fantasies might be off center or that Avey is content with her life. At this juncture, the narrator begins a lengthy series of idealized fantasies concerning his future relationship with Avey. He believes himself to be her heroic savior. At some point, he will rescue her from her indifference and sexual impropriety.

Section Two begins with the narrator regretting Avey's indifference to him. He attempts to impress her in a typical manner by showing off his athletic prowess in basketball, drill, swimming, and finally, dancing. She is not visibly impressed. He does make some breakthrough on an excursion to Riverview Amusement Park. At last Avey begins to notice his attentiveness. In a highly romantic setting, on the top deck of the *Jane Mosely*, the narrator finds himself alone with Avey. He begins to assume the Prufrock manner here as "do I dare?" creeps into his mind. He wants a passionate tryst and gives her "one burning kiss."[46] Instead of returning his passion, she places him on her lap and begins humming a lullaby. He is helpless to kindle a sexual response, or so he says. They converse but all the while his thoughts are on her sensuality: "Her eyes were soft and misty, the curves of her lips wistful...."[47] Unfortunately, the more he talks the less interested she becomes. The narrator does not realize it but he has inadvertently exposed the contrast between their concepts of life. He anticipates, intellectualizes, and becomes paralyzed by inaction. In contrast, Avey experiences the moment in carpe-diem fashion. She drinks of the atmosphere.

Section Three begins at Harper's Ferry one year later, a year lost in the pursuit of Avey. They are again in a romantic setting called Lover's Leap. The sensory images here are primarily aural as opposed to olfactory in Section One. The narrator recalls the sound of trains moving in the valley below, relating them to Avey. "The engines of the valley have a whistle, the echoes of which sound like iterated gasps and solos. I always think of them as crude music from Avey."[48] Again, he fails to arouse Avey's sensuality because of his inaction. He does touch her breast but goes no further even though they will spend many evenings at Lover's Leap. Almost imperceptibly, the narrator's attitude begins to change toward Avey. He begins to nourish a sense of superiority. According to him, Avey is guilty of "... downright laziness, sloppy indolence." Toomer inserts some schoolgirl humor here as the narrator calls Avey a cow since the narrator believes her breasts have the same texture as udders he felt on Wisconsin cows while he was in agricultural school there. This air of superiority continues. The narrator thrusts Avey from his mind for two years after which he receives a letter from her. Avey informs him that "she had lost her school and was going away."[49] Rather than sympathize with Avey, the narrator takes pains to criticize her poor penmanship and sloppy stationery. He returns to Washington now of the opinion that Avey is a whore, unworthy of his attention.

Section Four begins some five years later. The narrator admittedly remains haunted by visions of Avey even though he maintains a patronizing attitude toward her life-style. He begins an odyssey of sorts, attempting to find his lost Avey. By chance, he runs into her one lovely June evening on U Street. Still beautiful, Avey is walking with a gentleman friend. Shortly thereafter, the companion jumps into a cab, leaving Avey standing on the curb. The narrator suggests they they go to the park. Although he is relieved and encouraged by his reunion with Avey, the narrator demonstrates the same attitude toward her as he did at the conclusion of Section Two. He describes Avey as "indolent," and her eyes as being "indifferent." The reader strikes a different attitude toward the narrator. He truly believes himself superior even though during the five years away from Avey, he admittedly has accomplished little of substance. He remains paralyzed by inaction.

The fifth and final section begins as Avey and the narrator arrive at Soldier's Home, a park overlooking Washington proper. Once again, the narrator takes great pains to describe the romantic setting, emphasizing elements of the landscape. "And when the wind is from the South, soil of my homeland folks like a fertile shower upon the lean streets of the city." The direct reference to loss of roots and nostalgia for the South is a thematic consideration not lost on the reader but its significance is lost on the narrator. Toomer sacrifices the lack of perception and depth in the narrator. He is guilty of precisely what he accuses Avey of being. Toomer accomplishes this lifting of the veil technique here by having the narrator take great pains to impress the reader with his control over the situation. He lets it be known that he is an intimate acquaintance with the park guard. Therefore, the guard lets the couple alone. True to form, the narrator allows their possibilities for physical intimacy to fade. He begins a long internal monologue, the substance of which is a rehashing of his development and hers: "I traced my development from the early days up to the present time, the phase in which I could understand her. I described her own nature and temperament. Told how they needed a larger life for their expression."[50] The key phrase in this summary is "phase in which I could understand her." Obviously he does not understand Avey and the rest of his rhetoric is stripped away in light of this insight. Never content, he replaces his own failures by implying that Avey has not reached as far as he has and lacks the vision to realize her full potential.

Abruptly, the narrator changes moods. He becomes hostile and accusatory. He resents her laziness since she has not returned his professed affection. She is indifferent to his philosophical statements and abstractions. In fact, she has fallen asleep. The narrator lies there for hours, finally covering her with a blanket as the Washington dawn approaches. He compares her face to that dawn: "She did not have the gray crimson-splashed beauty of the dawn."[51] Her beauty is fading or is it that the narrator's view of her beauty if losing its perception. Toomer allows this ambiguity to slip by the narrator. The narrative ends with his solemn summary that Avey is an "orphan woman."

Toomer evidently intended "Avey" to be a touchstone, linking this section to the earlier stories, particularly the ones dominated by female characterizations. "Rhobert," the preceding narrative, also forms a thematic link to "Avey." Toomer is quite successful with the format since there are correlations to "Karintha," "Fern," and the stilted, sterile rhetoric Rhobert employs to the same end as the narrator of "Avey." Toomer also places emphasis on two motifs in "Avey": the theme of blindness and the use of trees in symbolic fashion.

The narrator is blind to his own inadequacies and certainly blind to the true beauty and character of Avey. He is also blind to the natural feelings he takes such care to suppress. The separate settings in the last three sections of "Avey" are romantic enough in themselves but the narrator cannot see such potential in the landscape. Finally, the narrator is blind to his own insight or rather lack of it. He views the world through a very narrow perspective, thus limiting his own vision of himself and especially his view of Avey.

The use of trees in "Avey" as symbols is not so readily clear. Arlene Crewdson correctly notes the relationship between the motif of blindness and the tree imagery. She states that the narrator "sees himself and Avey as like the young trees held in and stunted by their boxes on the Washington streets, but although the narrator may hack at the boxes, he can never free the trees."[52] In effect, the narrator does not realize he is blind to the relevance of the analogy to their relationship. Like the boxed trees, he has categorized Avey, leaving her with no room to expand. This is also an indirect reference to the symbolic use of the box seat in the story of the same name and in "Theatre" where one is also limited by point of view and reference. The motifs of blindness and boxed trees serve Toomer's purpose well here.

The style of this sketch is much weaker, or perhaps we may say, much less effective than in many of Toomer's other sketches and stories. Though the tone of the piece would lead us to expect long, meandering, and monotonous sentences, actually the style, especially that of the opening scenes, is monotonous in that the author uses series of short, matter-of-fact statements that contribute nothing toward the building up of the narrator's passion for Avey. Hence, this sketch lacks the force of some of the earlier pieces in which the author's language contributes greatly to the reader's final impression. Some of the scenes, it is true, do contain fine descriptive passages, notably the first few scenes in which girls are compared to young trees in boxes: "The young trees had not outgrown their boxes then....I like to feel that something deep in me responded to the trees, the young trees that whinnied like colts impatient to be let free." Yet the sketch remains the weakest in *Cane*.

XI *"Theatre"*

In one of the sketches about the dazzling night life of the city, "Theatre," Toomer presents two class-conscious blacks who are unable to approach each other because of differences in social status. There is a barrier between the two because of respectability: stage people are not considered respectable, whereas audiences are. John, a theater-manager's brother, and Dorris, a chorus girl employed there, are mutually attracted, but each approaches the other only in a dream fantasy. John's social status as a university-educated man and as a very light black from the city convinces Dorris that he is "dictie" (an epithet Toomer applies to people who are conscious of their social class, such as light-skinned blacks or professional blacks). Dorris evidences her pride by the only art at her command, dancing, and she dances in hopes of winning him. Dorris dances spontaneously at rehearsal, and to John, who watches her from the audience, her singing and dancing seem to be of "canebrake loves and mangrove feastings." Dorris is a bit of "black-skinned life" which permeates the walled-in life of the confines of the city. While John watches her at the rehearsals, Dorris sees him and senses that he might be someone who could offer her a family and a home life, but she is deterred in her thoughts about him when her dancing partner assures her that he is "dictie." Dorris, however, throws herself so unconsciously into the dance routine that she draws the admiration of onlookers even from the alleyways. John is visibly affected by the high emotional quality of Dorris's dance and momentarily he loses himself in the reverie of an imagined affair with her and begins to dream of her:

The walls press in, singing. Flesh of a throbbing body, they press close to John and Dorris. They close them in. John's heart beats tensely against her dancing body. Walls press his mind within his heart. And then, the shaft of light goes out the window high above him. John's mind sweeps up to follow it. Mind pulls him upward into dream. Dorris dances...John dreams.[53]

Though Dorris and John unite only in an imagined sort of animal ecstasy, Dorris feels this union and expects John to make some overture to her. Instead of responding, John takes refuge in a dream. "Walls press his mind within his heart." He escapes the reality of his own passion. As he dreams, Dorris looks at John and mistakes the passiveness of dreaming in his face for indifference, and she whirls off the dance floor. Had either John or Dorris been able to bridge the social distance between them, a satisfying relationship might have developed. This social distance is dual in nature: one an artificial separation and the other inherent in the nature of beings. Likewise, the title "Theatre" seems to signify the distance between the theater and real life.

Toomer makes it clear that personal communication is essential to any relationship. Throughout the narrative, neither Dorris nor John actually talks to the other. John represses his physical desires since he is an "actor" playing the role of intellectual. John fails to recognize that physical and intellectual development can coincide meaningfully. In fact, the more John rationalizes his relationship and beliefs about Dorris, about whom he actually knows little, the more he muddles the real Dorris. Instead of possessing her, he grabs one of his manuscripts and begins reading. She fades from his thoughts and from the narrative. "Theatre" in theme and character elicits Toomer's basic theme in Section Two. Blacks who live in urban areas like Washington, D.C. have lost some naturalness, an element prevalent in the Georgian section.

XII *"Box Seat"*

"Box Seat" is probably the sketch in which Toomer's theme of man's being constricted by modern society is most obviously evident. The protagonist is Dan Moore, a young black who believes himself to be destined to heal a sick world that has been confined by society. He says, "I am Dan Moore. I was born in a canefield. The hands of Jesus touched me. I am come to a sick world to heal it."[54] Blacks, Dan says, are "withered people" who need to be called from their houses (a confinement symbol) and taught to dream.

Dan is in love with Muriel, a schoolteacher, and when he goes to see her, he becomes exceedingly aware of the conventions that are restraining her and keeping her, and other people as well, in bonds.

While Dan is waiting for Muriel, he imagines that he is a representative of the underground races sent to free the world:

Dan goes to the wall and places his ear against it. A passing street car and something vibrant from the earth sends a rumble to him. That rumble comes from the earth's deep core. It is the mutter of powerful underground races. Dan has a picture of all the people rushing to put their ears against walls, to listen to it. The next world-saviour is coming that way. Coming up. A continent sinks down. The new-world Christ will need consummate skill to walk upon the waters where huge bubbles burst.[55]

Dan feels the stricture of confinement about Muriel also:

Dan rises. His arms stretch towards her. His fingers and his palms, pink in the lamplight, are glowing irons. Muriel's chair is close and stiff about her. The house, the rows of houses locked about her chair. Dan's fingers and arms are fire to melt and bars to wrench and force and pry. Her arms hang loose. Her hands are hot and moist.[56]

Dan believes that he, having been "born in a canefield," has felt the hands of Jesus touch him and that he is equipped to free Muriel and the whole world.

Muriel, who is the symbol of conventionality, lives in a world of restrictions. As a schoolteacher, her conduct is guided by moral codes of the community. For instance, in the home of Mrs. Pribby, with whom she lives, she is constantly in fear of her conduct being unseemly. After a love scene between Muriel and Dan, Mrs. Pribby raps on a newspaper to obtain quiet and Muriel "fastens on her image"—that of a schoolteacher. Mrs. Pribby seems to be the projection of Muriel and her adherence to the established social and moral codes of behavior for teachers. Later in her box seat at the theater, Muriel is under observation by the stage performers, by the audience, and also by Dan, who has entered later and has seated himself where he can scrutinize her. Muriel feels that she is being confined by the seats of the theater:

Each one is a bolt that shoots into a slot, and is locked there....The seats are slots. The seats are bolted houses. The mass grows denser. Its weight at first is impalpable upon the box. Then Muriel begins to feel it. She props her arm against the brass-rail, to ward it off.[57]

The box-seat symbol is a continuation of the house symbol, which Toomer uses to show how society and the mechanized world have constricted men so that they have built up inhibitions.

Toomer created Dan to project his own belief that men have been enslaved by modern mechanistic society. Once, just before his enlightening trip to Georgia, he had said in a letter to Lola Ridge:

It would surprise you to see the anemia and the timidity (emotional) in folks but a generation or so removed from the Negroes of the folk-songs. Full blooded people to look at who are afraid to hold hands, much less love.[58]

Muriel, as Toomer says, is afraid to hold hands or to love. Dan recognizes this and believes that his closeness to the soil has rendered him capable of being a savior to those like her who are confined as she is confined by society. Consequently, he is irritated by people who observe so faithfully the restrictions of society. From his seat in the theater, Dan can watch Muriel as she seems to be locked in her box-seat, and he thinks to himself: "He-slave. Slave of a woman who is a slave." Muriel, too, feels that she is confined by her position and she fidgets in the seat and turns her head away from Dan. Dan, meanwhile, is sitting next to a portly black woman who symbolizes the person who still has roots in the South, close to the soil. He thinks of her:

A soil-soaked fragrance comes from her. Through the cement floor her strong roots sink down. They spread under the asphalt streets. Dreaming, the streets roll over their bellies, and suck their glossy health from them. Her strong roots sink down and spread under the river and disappear in blood-lines that waver south. Her roots shoot down. Dan's hand follows them. Roots throb. Dan's heart beats violently. He places his palms upon the earth to cool them. Earth throbs. Dan's heart beats violently. He sees all the people rush to the walls to listen to the rumble. A new-world Christ is coming up. Dan comes up. He is startled. The eyes of the woman don't belong to her. They look at him unpleasantly. From either aisle, bolted masses press in. He doesn't fit. The mass grows agitant. For an instant, Dan's and Muriel's eyes meet.[59]

Muriel has shunned Dan in the theater because she does not believe that he is aggressive enough in life and because he does not fit into her world of conventionality. She asks him why he does not get a job and settle down. At the theater, she sees him enter and realizes that he may embarrass her. She tries to convince herself that she does not love him and that her actions will keep him from daring to approach her in public. At her home, she had been able to rebuff him only with the help of Mrs. Pribby.

The vaudeville show which is presented reconfirms the main theme that society has enslaved people. The performers of the main attraction are two grotesque dwarfs who fight each other aimlessly yet furiously. Their fight is a symbol of the complete deterioration of mechanized society. The champion of the ludicrous fray singles out Muriel and offers her a rose which she reluctantly accepts. Dan, when Muriel accepts the dwarf's rose, is aware of her deceit because she accepts the rose from the dwarf but has rebuffed him. He becomes hysterical; he imagines that he will demolish the building (and all other means of confinement in society), and will arise and save the world. Dan leaves the theater, having thrown off the shackles of Muriel's love, and offends a theater patron, who challenges him to a fight. Dan, however, is free of the hold that both Muriel and society have on him: "He is as cool as a green stem that has just shed its flower." The faces around him become impalpable and he disregards them. He walks away, free, from theater, from Muriel, and from society. "Box Seat" and "Theatre" are companion pieces. Dan and Muriel are contrapuntal to John and Dorris.

Toomer firmly believed that the black peasant's alienation from the soil had caused him to become emotionally sterile. His trip to Georgia, which gave him the fundamental groundwork for *Cane*, convinced him that he might find in racial substance something distinctive which should be a genuine contribution to art. He believed that slavery, once considered the black's shame and stigma, was a source of growth and transfiguration. As he said in his poem "Song of the Son," "One plum was saved for me; one seed becomes/An everlasting song, a singing tree/Carolina softly souls of slavery."[60]

XIII *"Calling Jesus"*

"Calling Jesus" is a very short sketch, but it contains the central theme of the entire group of selections. It concerns an urbanized woman who has moved to the city and has developed the "anemia and emotional timidity" to which Toomer has referred. Enclosed in a big house in the city, she becomes estranged from her soul, which the narrator likens to a little thrust-tailed dog that follows her continually. Like the whimpering dog which is kept out of the house by a huge storm door, so is her soul kept from her body by the barriers erected by the city environment. Her eyes seem to have a longing for a place where builders find "no need for vestibules, for swinging on iron hinges, storm doors," where she not confined by life away from the soil, the narrator is saying, her soul would not lack expression. He concludes:

Her soul is like a little thrust-tailed dog, that follows her, whimpering. I've seen it tagging on behind her, up streets where chestnut trees flowered, where dusty asphalt had been freshly sprinkled with clean water. Up alleys where niggers sat on low doorsteps before tumbled shanties and sang and loved. At night, when she comes home, the little dog is left in the vestibule, nosing the crack beneath the big storm door, filled with chills till morning. Some one . . . echo Jesus . . . soft as the bare feet of Christ moving across bales of southern cotton, will steal in and cover it that it need not shiver, and carry it to her where she sleeps: cradled in dream-fluted cane.[61]

XIV "Rhobert"

The second selection and first narrative in Section Two of *Cane* is "Rhobert." Its placement as an introductory sketch is deliberate and "Rhobert" encompasses the rootless urban characterizations which Toomer stresses in this section. Rhobert himself is a product of urban life, a life which results in massive sterility of mind and spirit. Hence, by extension, Rhobert is representative of a fatal removal from the soil, a loss of roots, which becomes the overriding symbol throughout the contrapuntal "Northern" section of *Cane*.

"Rhobert" is more an analysis and a philosophic treatise than a piece of short fiction. It consists of three paragraphs, the last two reiterating symbols and moralizing described in the first paragraph. In a tight, complex style, the narrator describes the character of Rhobert and his elemental losses as a materialistic being. Rhobert "wears a house, like a monstrous diver's helmet, on his head."[62] That is, material values and objects weigh Rhobert down, stifling his humanity. "He is way down." Apparently this image is linked to the "weighted down" element of the house on his head. "He is sinking. This house is a dead thing that weighs him down."[63] The house becomes the central metaphor in "Rhobert." It is an excellent metaphorical vehicle since the reader can identify the house with materialistic values, the boxed in intellect, and finally, appreciate the burden of objects which so many aspire to have. The word play with head of household is further evidence of the metaphor's usefulness. In this instance the head of the house is literally in view.

The image of Rhobert carrying a house on his head is quite evidently surrealistic. It's not unlike the extended metaphor used by Kafka in *Metamorphosis*. In fact, Rhobert's house has rods protruding "like antennae" and the house is described as being "like a monstrous helmet," similar to the carapace of an insect like Kafka's protagonist. The philosophic stance in "Rhobert" is similar to the more direct criticism Thoreau employs in the "Economy" section of *Walden*. Moreover, T. S. Eliot's "The Hollow Men" invites comparison to "Rhobert" since Toomer also inserts the "straw" and "stuffed" elements to his description of Rhobert's house.

The narrator reiterates Rhobert's description and plight in paragraphs two and three of the selection. Rhobert is a product of his own making. He cares more for the house than he does his family since "he cares not two straws as to whether or not he will ever see his wife and children again."[64] Eventually, the sheer weight of the house will drag him down and Rhobert will disappear in the mind. The narrator believes that his contemporaries will place a monument over the spot, "a monument of hewn oak, carved in nigger-heads." Toomer solidifies his intentions for "Rhobert" with his description of a suitable monument. It is these uprooted blacks whom he uses as the primary subjects in Section Two. Out of their element, they will fall victim to society's materialism as surely as Rhobert does. When Rhobert "goes down" under the ooze, the narrator will join in the singing of "Deep River." The narrative ends with the poetic

> Brother, Rhobert is sinking.
> Let's open our throats, brother,
> Let's sing Deep River when he goes down.[65]

"Deep River" is a soul-opening spiritual, praising the natural elements so akin to and necessary for humanity. It is an appropriate death knell, recalling the price Rhobert pays for removing himself from his natural state. Rhobert's final resting place will be a wasteland, a monument with serious implications in itself.

Darwin Turner made a rather profound statement regarding Toomer's motivations for Section Two of *Cane* and it readily applies to "Rhobert." Turner noted that after Section One was completed, "Jean Toomer the lyricist was dying; Jean Toomer the philosopher and psychologist reformer was coming into being."[66]

Henceforth, as "Rhobert" demonstrates, *Cane* becomes less a fictive work than a philosophical one. Rhobert "is the apex of modern dehumanized man who is drowning in his own materialistic values."[67] Modern men, rootless men, like Rhobert are guilty of spiritual decadence. Toomer even describes his God in satirical fashion. "God is a Red Cross man with a dredge and a respirator-pump who's waiting for you at the opposite periphery."[68] It is precisely the image needed to describe the end result of such spiritual decadence.

XV *"Bona and Paul"*

"Bona and Paul," the last story of the second section of *Cane*, represents the awakening of a young mulatto to the consciousness of his race. This story initiates the next turning of the thematic circle, which Toomer has structured as a complete circle beginning with the awakening of the black to his racial dilemma. In a letter to Waldo Frank, written while he was working on the volume, he said of this plan:

From three angles, *Cane*'s design is a circle. Aesthetically, from simple forms to complex ones, and back to simple forms. Regionally from South up to North, and back into the South again. Or, from the North down into the South, and then a return North. From the point of view of the spiritual entity behind the work, the curve really starts with "Bona and Paul" (awakening), plunges into "Kabnis," emerges in "Karintha," etc., swings upward into "Theatre" and "Box Seat" and ends (pauses) in "Harvest Song."[69]

This awakening of Paul and Bona to the racial dilemma in which they are enmeshed is the major problem of these two young people. Paul, a Southerner and a mulatto, has enrolled in the University of Chicago and has become friendly with Bona, a young white student. She has fallen in love with Paul, even though she is aware that he is possibly a black. Bona, from the South, finds that in Chicago, Paul's racial identity is negligible as a factor in her love for him. Though the dormitory girls and his roommate all question whether or not Paul is a black, Paul has never committed himself. Bona remains, however, exceedingly attracted to Paul and seeks at every opportunity to be in his presence. She attributes her attraction to him to the rumor that dark-skinned men are fascinating. Though the other girls in the dormitory, the waiters in the restaurants, and black doormen all cast knowing looks at the couple, indicating that they suspect that Paul is a black, Bona's desire to have him acknowledge his love for her is firm. Paul, however, finds that his mind keeps wandering back to his heritage. He thinks of his Georgia home:

Paul follows the sun, over the stock-yards where a fresh stench is just arising, across wheat lands that are still waving above their stubble, into the sun. Paul follows the sun to a pine-matted hillock in Georgia. He sees the slanting roofs of gray unpainted cabins tinted lavender. A Negress chants a lullaby beneath the mate-eyes of a southern planter. Her breasts are ample for the suckling of a song. She weans it, and sends it, curiously waving, among lush melodies of cane and corn. Paul follows the sun into himself in Chicago.[70]

This dedication is particularly relevant to Toomer's intent for the narrative and whole of Section Two. The passage reinforces Paul's nostalgia—his remembrance of the fertile Georgia landscape and the heritage owed to those natural roots. Toomer contrasts the fertility of the Georgia setting with the sterility of Chicago: the stock yards give off a "fresh stench," but his love resounds with "lush melodies of cane and corn." When Paul "follows the sun into himself in Chicago," he develops an internalized view of the past. That is, Paul keeps his racial memories intact but does not verbalize them in "Bona and Paul." This is one of the hazards of urban migration. So far removed from a natural surrounding, Paul can identify only with the sun, not with the stench of the city.

Paul becomes moody and distant as he thinks about coming to know Bona fully. But Paul's intellectual thirst takes precedence over his love for her. He knows that Bona comes from the South, where her attitudes toward blacks ought to be hostile, and he consequently believes that her makeup would be such that he could never come to know her fully. As he keeps dreaming of the "color and the music and the song" of his race, he recognizes that the distance between the two of them is too great to bridge the gap. In the final scene when another black stares at him, indicating that he knows his racial identity, Paul, in a moment of release from his attraction to the white girl, shakes the black's hand, tells him that he is going back to the dark faces that he may really know and in which he finds beauty that is "purple like a bed of roses would be at dusk." Bona, too, has recognized the spiritual gulf between her and Paul and has fled from him.

"Bona and Paul" is divided into four sections. The first section is devoted to an impressionistic study of Bona. The setting is a gymnasium where various physical exercises are taking place, including drill and basketball. Bona, as observer, describes Paul: "He is a candle that dances in a grove swaying with pole balloons." It is a rather strained metaphor but the poetic element is not Toomer's primary concern. Just as Paul will shortly reminisce about his Georgia roots, Bona recalls the prom setting of her adolescence. It is a remarkable contrast between the shanty and the upper class gala atmosphere. In an even more revealing comment which follows, Bona describes Paul as a "harvest moon," "an autumn leaf," and "a nigger." It is an abrupt revelation, the single over-riding fact in "Bona and Paul." Because of his race, Paul's physical and spiritual beauty is muted. Nevertheless, Bona becomes a participant in the basketball game rather than a spectator. She wants to be close to Paul, perhaps even to impress him. She guards Paul too closely and is cracked in the jaw with his elbow. He grabs her before she can fall. She stiffens with the initial physical contact "then becomes strangely vibrant, and bursts to a swift life within her anger." Paul senses her reluctance but a passion stirs within him, especially after Bona squeezes him. Paul becomes aware of the circle of staring faces, as does Bona. She jerks herself free and flees. Toomer creates a credible atmosphere of tension. Even though Bona and Paul momentarily become physically attractive, the strain of a black man holding a white girl becomes unbearable. The use of the word "whir" is significant. There is a whir of activity.

Section Two is devoted to Paul's perspective. He lives in a room beside a railroad track. There are two windows in Paul's room: "Bona is one window. One window Paul." Racial ambivalence is symbolized by these windows: "Through one he sees his roots, reaching back to the hills of Georgia, and his heritage in the lullaby of the black woman singing under the lusting eyes of a southern planter. Yet at the second window, Bona's window, there is only blackness."[71] Paul is "passing" for white but the tension he feels begins to mount and will increase as the narrative progresses. The second section continues with the introduction of Paul's roommate Art, who is as uncertain of Paul's racial makeup as the rest. Art has "fixed up" Paul with a date. He is anxious for them to be on their way to dinner at the Pine Food Restaurant. Art and his girl, Helen, are going on a double date with Paul and Bona to the Crimson Gardens.

In Section Three, Toomer develops his characterizations by placing them in situational difficulties. Art is well dressed, bubbling over with anticipation. Conversely, Paul is "cool like the dusk, and like the dusk, detached." The girls arrive. Art and Helen continue an argument "where he had last left it." Bona squeezes Paul's hand but suddenly feels the same kind of tension she felt on the basketball court. In order to control her emotions, Bona "flares to poise and security." On the way to Crimson Gardens, Bona asks Paul to tell her about himself, implying that he reveal his racial identity. But she only wants to know what he wants to tell her. Paul sidesteps her question, remarking that she has "the beauty of a gem fathoms under sea." Bona professes love for Paul. This gem, the jewel, is cast into Paul's hand. Paul cannot speak of love. He wants physical proof from Bona because "love is a dry rain in my mouth unless it is wet with kisses." Bona pulls Paul to her but stiffens again as in the gymnasium. She wants acknowledgment of love from Paul. He cannot make such an acknowledgment and accuses Bona of being cold.

The final section of "Bona and Paul" might properly be called the "Crimson Gardens." Paul recedes into his shell, oblivious of the gala atmosphere of the surroundings. He feels self-conscious among all the white faces. Toomer uses window imagery to emphasize Paul's mood. He is "rosy before the window" and "with his own glow, he seeks to penetrate a dark pane," Bona. He cannot yet reveal his concerns and attempts to become one of the revelers. "Crimson Gardens is a body where blood flows to a clot upon the dance floor." Art and Helen are clots as well as Paul and Bona. As they dance, the conversation turns somewhat sour. Bona accuses Paul of being too cold, rational, and philosophic. She tries to move away from Paul in disgust, lest he grab her in much the same manner as he did in the gymnasium. "They are a dizzy blood clot on a gymnasium floor."

The story ends rather abruptly when Paul and Bona leave the dance. They encounter a huge black uniformed doorman whom Paul engages in a revealing conversation. He says,

I came back to tell you, to shake your hand, and tell you that you are wrong. That something beautiful is going to happen. That the Gardens are purple like a bed of roses would be at dusk. That I came into the Garden, into life in the Gardens with one whom I did not know. That I danced with her, and did not know her. That I felt passion, contempt and passion for her whom I did not know. That I thought of her. That my thoughts were matches thrown into a dark window.[72]

Paul makes the conscious choice to become more intimate with Bona; the white world is his destiny. But as he turns he discovers that Bona has disappeared. Toomer's implication here is that Paul cannot know another until he knows himself. There is little chance that Paul will have this opportunity for self-knowledge since he has cut himself off from the Georgia roots. "Bona and Paul" ends on a negative note, consistent with the theme of lost heritage of subsequent sterility in Section Two of *Cane*.

Thus, the second section of *Cane* continues the aesthetic circle and treats blacks who are in sharp contrast to those of Section One. The primitives of the Georgia Pike of Section One, whose natural impulses have felt no sense of confinement, have experienced the beauty of life. As blacks move to city environments, where they are enclosed by houses, asphalt streets, and the smugness associated with the rising bourgeoisie, they lose their souls, as did the woman whose soul resembled a "little thrust-tailed dog." Constrained by society, they constantly attempt, as Muriel of "Box Seat" does, to "fasten on an image." Section Three continues the circle by recording the reactions of blacks to the various pressures of Southern environment, and analyzing the reaction of a Northern born and educated black to that of an old ex-slave who has been completely dehumanized.

XVI *Section Three: "Kabnis"*

The structural, aesthetic, and thematic circle of *Cane* is completed by a return to the South. The third section, a novella entitled "Kabnis," is an adaptation of Toomer's drama by the same name. This section of *Cane* approaches the problem of the black, not by an acute analysis of the issues faced by the black, but by a poignant revelation of the feelings of a black whose chief concern is the aesthetic. In Section Three the protagonist is a Northerner who has returned to the home of his ancestors in the South to enjoy the beauty he hopes to find there. Like the poet in "Song of the Son," Kabnis is a son of the soil returned to the land of his ancestors for the purpose of enjoying the aesthetic of the land and the red soil. But the neurotic lyricist, seeking beauty in a land that is filled with ugliness, cannot come to grips with the traditions of his slave heritage.

Ralph Kabnis is a Northerner of mixed blood. He returns to his family home in order to recapture a lost sense of self. He is the sum of the lost sould in *Cane* who precede him. His case is all the more gripping because he represents the ultimate danger of prejudice and its divisive results. At the end of the narration, Ralph has replaced the substance of manhood with the mere shadow of his former self.

Ralph Kabnis is overwhelmed by the beauty of the South but, to this frustrated poet, beauty becomes ugliness because he cannot endure the humiliation that blacks are forced to accept. He wonders how blacks can farm, sing, love, and sleep in the South and remain content with such a life. "This loneliness, dumbness, awful intangible oppression is enough to drive a man insane," he says as he contemplates the school he is forced to teach in under the direction of Hanby, the autocratic principal. He is disturbed because he can see "white minds, with indolent assumption, juggle justice and nigger." He sees the South as a place where blacks have been relegated to a position of ugliness in the midst of beauty; consequently, he finds it difficult to identify himself with the Georgia landscape. Blacks, he knows, are cut off from the beauty of the South because whites are in control. He hears the weird chill of the Georgia winds say: "White man's land./Niggers, sing./Burn, bear black childen/Till poor rivers bring/Rest, and sweet glory/In Camp Ground."[73]

He finds that the restrictions placed upon him as a schoolteacher are inconsistent. For instance, under the code of unwritten law, he is not allowed to smoke, yet in the South, "they burn a nigger," he says. He sees himself as "going bats" because of the loneliness forced upon him in the South. Kabnis, after listening to blacks' harrowing accounts of actual lynchings, develops a fear of lynching that completely unnerves him. At night, he comes to fear every small sound of nature and associates these with possible lynch mobs. This fear, as well as frustrating restrictions placed on Southern blacks, drown his ability to put into written lyrical expression his reactions to the "face of the South." He is overcome by a "weird chill."

In the process of his degradation, Kabnis touches various aspects of his black heritage, none of which serves to stabilize his neurotic despair. From the blacks whom he encounters, he is unable to gain any encouragement because all of them have in some way or other been detrimentally affected by the social traditions of the South. Toomer offers an indictment of the Southern educational system by his portrait of Samuel Hanby, the overbearing black principal in whose school Kabnis is forced to work, and in his description of Halsey, who is an exponent of the Booker T. Washington school of educational thought. Hanby, the principal of the training school for blacks, is the "Uncle Tom" representative of the whites among blacks. The school of which he is, as he says, the "humble president," is obviously operated like a plantation, with Hanby as the overseer. Hanby has maintained a semblance of respect among whites because he spends his money with them. With blacks, however, he assumes a haughty, superior, Puritanical air, and reminds them frequently of his position of leadership in the community. When he comes to dismiss Kabnis, he delivers him an oration, meant to impress his listeners:

Hum. Erer, Professor Kabnis, to come straight to the point: the progress of the Negro race is jeopardized whenever the personal habits and examples set by its guides and mentors fall below the acknowledged and hard-won standard of its average member. This institution, of which I am the humble president, was founded, and has been maintained at a cost of great labor and untold sacrifice. Its purpose is to teach our youth to live better, cleaner, more noble lives. To prove to the world that the Negro race can be just like any other race. It hopes to attain this aim partly by the salutary examples set by its instructors. I cannot hinder the progress of a race simply to indulge a single member. I have thought the matter out beforehand, I can assure you. Therefore, if I find your resignation on my desk tomorrow morning, Mr. Kabnis, I shall not feel obliged to call in the sheriff. Otherwise . . . . [74]

After his dismissal, Kabnis is befriended by Halsey, who becomes one of the stabilizing forces in his deep slope downward. Halsey, who operates a small repair shop that caters to both white and black customers, has not been completely crushed by Southern life. He has simply accommodated his life to the prevailing ideals of the white South. He undergoes the indignities of the South by being somewhat of a servant to whites—and to some few blacks. Escaping into a sort of self-satisfaction by following the traditional path laid out for blacks, Halsey exists as an independent laborer. He advocates the cast-down-your-bucket-where-you philosophy of Booker T. Washington, which discourages blacks from following intellectual pursuits and favors their working with their hands at simple trades. He believes that an occupational trade is the only way a man can obtain soul satisfaction. He says:

Give me th work and fair pay and I aint askin nothin better. Went overseas and saw France; an I come back . . . Went to school; but there aint no books whats got the feel t them of them there tools. Nassur. An I'm a tellin y[72]

Halsey's reaction to the Southern community is bred in his bones.
Whereas the "ways of white folks" have frustrated Kabnis, Halsey
has been reduced to a shadow of a complete man. He is easily
intimidated; yet his very submission to the Southern way of life is
his salvation—a salvation which Kabnis can never achieve because
he refuses to allow himself to be completely subdued spiritually.
Halsey is content to "stand in the doorway and gaze up the street
expectantly," hoping for jobs to come to him, but Kabnis rebels
against the apathy of this type of black who has no incentive to be
independent of white domination. Though Halsey, too, is an "Uncle
Tom," he does not tyrannize his fellow blacks as Hanby does.
Halsey is condescendingly humble with whites, but with blacks he
becomes militant. When Hanby irritates him by his dismissal of
Kabnis, he threatens him:

Let me get you told right now, Mr. Samuel Hanby. Now listen t me. I aint
no slick and span slave youve hired, an dont y think it for a minute. Youve
bullied enough about this town. An besides, wheres that bill youve been
owin me. Listen t me. If I dont get it paid in by tmorrer noon, Mr. Hanby
(he mockingly assumes Hanby's tone and manner), I shall feel obliged t call
the sheriff. An that sheriff'll be myself who'll catch y in the road and pull y
out your buggy and rightly attent t y. You heard me. Now leave him alone.
I'm takin him home with me. I got it fixed. He's goin to work with me.
Shapin shafts and buildin wagons'll make a man of him what nobody, y get
me? what nobody can take advantage of. Thats all....[76]

Thus the militancy left in Halsey's spirit, after partial dehumanizing
by his life in the South, is reserved for black underlings. Toward
Hanby, the educated black, he assumes a superior air, but he is
protective of Kabnis and tries to show him how to readjust himself
by following what, for blacks, is the best course—that of not
competing with whites intellectually. His philosophy toward
Kabnis, blacks as well, is indicated in his final statement to Hanby:
"Shapin shafts and buildin wagons'll make a man of him what
nobody...can take advantage of."[77] Halsey has not allowed his life
as a Southern black to become painful. He had adjusted himself to
the life there and reorganized his talents according to the privileges
accorded him by Southern society.

Layman, who "knows more than is good for anyone except a
silent man," also represents the voice of the Southern black. He is
Georgia born and educated, by turns a teacher and a preacher. He
has traveled widely in the South, has studied black-white psychology

and he tells Kabnis: "Nigger's a nigger down this away, Professor. An only two dividins: good an bad. An even they aint permanent categories. They sometimes mixes em up when it comes to lynchin. I've seen em do it."[78]

Like Halsey, who has accepted a life in the South which requires him to submit to numerous indignities, Layman suffers under the yoke of Southern white dominance, and assumes the air that his fate as a black is something which not he, nor any black man, can change. He never condemns whites; he simply adapts himself to the customs of the South.

Even Lewis, who might have served as a stabilizing force for Kabnis, is no help for him when he becomes disposed to react to the social predicament by resorting to debauchery and despair. Lewis is a Christ figure. He has a sense of direction and acts with intelligence whereas Kabnis lets his pent-up emotions guide his actions. As a character Lewis seems weak; yet Toomer seems to have so designed him for the purpose of making him represent the man that Kabnis could possibly have been if he had not allowed himself to be driven by his unconscious desires for the impossible. Kabnis consequently deteriorates while Lewis withstands the pressures of his environment by his Christ-like philosophy. Kabnis realizes Lewis's possible influence on him and the "licker," which released the conflicts in him, sets him to talking. He tells Lewis:

Know what's here. M soul. Ever heard o that? Th hell y have. Been shapin words t fit m soul. Never told y that before, did I? Thought I couldnt talk. I'll tell y. I've been shapin words; ah, but sometimes theyre beautiful an golden an have a taste that makes em fine t roll over with y tongue. Your tongue aint fit f nothing but t roll an lick hog-meat.[79]

Kabnis refuses to acknowledge his black heritage but Lewis accepts his. Lewis reminds Kabnis that the old man who is kept in the dark cellar of Halsey's place is symbolic of their black past. Kabnis denies his black heritage: "An besides, he aint my past. My ancestors were Southern bluebloods—." Kabnis the old man is a product of Uncle Tomism and a misused Christian religion. In the old man, Lewis sees strength which has come from the hardship and pain which he has suffered. Lewis chastizes Kabnis for not having accepted his black heritage as a part of his ancestry. He warns him that the white man is still master and that the black is his slave. Of whites, he tells Kabnis: "They fight and bastardize you...no use...."

In his downward plunge to debauchery, Kabnis also meets two black prostitutes at Halsey's shop, one of whom tells him the reasons for her fall:

A white man took m mother an it broke the old man's heart. He died; an then I didnt care what become of me, and I dont now. I dont care now. Dont get it in y head I'm some sentimental Susie askin for yo sop. Nassur. But there's somethin to yo th others aint got. Boars an kids and fools—that all I've known. Boars when their fever's up. When their fever's up they come t me.[80]

When she becomes reminiscent and tells Kabnis, "Usall is brought up t hate sin worse than death—," he replies aptly, "An then before you have y eyes half open, youre made t love it if y want t live."

Kabnis vents his hatred on Father John, the old ex-slave who is kept in the cold and dark cellar of Halsey's shop. Symbolic of the black's past, he is like the black's slave heritage that is kept hidden as a part of their lives not to be remembered. Living in quarters strongly resembling the hold of a slave ship, Father John sits as though chained to one spot, blind and almost inarticulate and capable only of mumbling in a tragic monotone his indictment against the white folks for the sin of slavery. "Th sin whats fixed...upon the white folks—....O the sins the white folks 'mitted when they made the bible lie," he would say. Kabnis, who cannot come to grips with the memory of his black heritage, projects his hatred toward the old man. He gushes out at him:

You sit there like a black hound spiked to an ivory pedestal. An all night long I heard you murmurin that devilish word. They thought I didnt hear y, but I did. Mumblin, feedin that ornery thing thats livin on my insides. Father John. Father of Satan, more likely. What does it mean t you? Youre dead already. Death. What does it mean t you? T you who died way back there in th sixties. What are y throwin it in my throat for? Whats it goin t get y? My fist'll sink in t y black mush face t y guts—if y got any. Dont believe y have. Never seen signs of none. Death. Death. Sin an Death. All night long y mumbled death....Death...these clammy floors...just like they used to stow away the worn out, no-count niggers in the days of slavery...that was long ago; not so long ago...no windows (he rises higher on his elbows to verify this assertion. He looks around, and seeing no one but the old man, calls.) Halsey! Halsey! Gone an left me. Just like a nigger. I thought he was a nigger all th time. Now I know it. Ditch y when it comes right down t it. Damn him anyway. Goddamn him. (He looks and resees the old man.) Eh, you? T hell with y too. What do I care whether you can see or hear? Y know what hell is cause you've been there. Its a feelin an its ragin in my soul in a way that'll pop out of me an run y through, an scorch y, an burn an rip your soul. Your soul. Ha. Nigger soul. A gin soul that gets drunk on a preacher's words. An screams. An shouts. God almighty, how I hate that shoutin. Where's the beauty in that? Gives a buzzard a windpipe an I'll bet a dollar t a dime th buzzard ud beat y to it. Aint suprisin th white folks hate y so. When you had eyes, did you ever see th beauty of th world? Tell me that. Th hell y did. Now don't tell me. I know y didnt. You couldnt have. Oh, I'm drunk an just as good as dead, but no eyes that have seen beauty ever lose their sight. You aint got no sight. If you had, drunk as I am, I hope Christ will kill me if I couldnt see it. Your eyes are dull and watery, like fish eyes. Fish eyes are dead eyes. Youre an old man, a dead fish man, an black at that. Theyve put y here t die, damn fool y are not t know it. Do y know how many feet youre under ground? I'll tell y. Twenty. And do y think you'll ever see th light of day again, even if you wasnt blind? Do y think youre out of slavery? Huh? Youre where they used t throw th worked-out, no-count slaves. On a damp clammy floor of a dark scum-hole. An they called that an infirmary. The sons-a . . . . Why I can already see you toppled off that stool an stretched out on th floor beside me—not beside me, damn you, by yourself, with th flies buzzin an lickin God knows what theyd find on a dirty, black, foul-breathed mouth like yours. . . .[81]

Thus, the old man represents the aspects of Kabnis's past that he wants to deny. Consequently Kabnis can only project his own self-hatred onto the old man. He hates him because of his lack of appreciation of the beauty which Kabnis is seeking for the South; he hates the old man's physical appearance and he hates the ties that the old man has with his slave past.

Lewis, but no Kabnis, recognizes that Carrie K., the adolescent sister of Halsey, symbolizes hope for blacks. Lewis sees immediately that her rich beauty and her spirit will fade, once she has been forced into the position of black women in the South. Toomer describes Lewis's meeting with Carrie K.:

Their meeting is a swift sunburst. Lewis impulsively moves toward her. His mind flashes images of her life in a southern town. He sees the nascent woman, her flesh already stiffening to cartilage, drying to bone. Her spirit-bloom, even now touched sullen, bitter. Her rich beauty fading. . . . He wants to—He stretches forth his hands to hers. He takes them. They feel like warm cheeks against his palms. The sunburst from her eyes floods up and haloes him. Christ-eyes, his eyes look to her. Fearlessly she loves into them. And then something happens. Her face blanches. Awkwardly she draws away. The sin-bogies of respectable southern colored folks clamor at her: "Look out! Be a *good* girl. Look out!"[82]

The dramatic novella ends with Kabnis having lost his complete dignity as he continues his descent into debauchery. His own self-hatred has been vented on everyone who represents any angle of vision of the black race, and he remains a confirmed coward in the face of his tradition. Kabnis, obviously almost white in appearance and in the outlook he wishes to adopt, is classified as a black. He revels in his own self-hatred, unable to find any outlet from his enforced position as a black. As a spokesman for the author Toomer, he represents two views toward the black race. On one hand, Kabnis sees beauty in the Georgia countryside which he cannot develop the complete freedom to enjoy or express in words. He also sees hope in Carrie K.—in the "calm untested confidence and nascent maturity which rise from her...mission," but Kabnis is not resurrected by the hope that she portrays. He cannot "merge with his source" as Lewis does. Instead, Kabnis sees, on the other hand, only loss of dignity and not strength and courage in the black, not even that arising from the old ex-slave's years of subjugation of whites. He can see nothing but shame and degradation in the acknowledgment of his black past. "Kabnis" reaffirms the theme of the first two sections of *Cane*, that there is beauty in the life of the Southern black but that the beauty that is there has been destroyed by confinement. In "Kabnis" the symbols of confinement are represented by the trade into which Halsey is forced, by the "sin-bogies" of which Carrie K. is constantly aware, by the educational system for which Hanby is the white man's spokesman, and by the pathological fear of lynching which Kabnis has developed.

Kabnis dreams of the South: "Night winds in Georgia are vagrant poets, whispering," but his dreams never become a reality because Kabnis is never able to "touch the soil." He thinks:

And dreams are faces with large eyes and weak chins and broad brows that get smashed by the fists of square faces. The body of the world is bullnecked. A dream is a soft face that fits uncertainly upon it....If I could feel that I came to the South to face it. If I, the dream (not what is weak and afraid in me) could become the face of the South. How my lips would sing for it, my songs being the lips of its soul.[83]

Thus, in "Kabnis" Toomer reaffirms his two views towards the black race, one of hope and one of self-hatred. Neither view is dominant with the protagonist Kabnis. His final position of despair is inevitable as he wavers between the lyrical beauty that he sees in the South and the hatred of his own self image.

The character Kabnis is a thinly disguised portrait of Toomer himself. Here is exemplified Toomer's need for a father figure and he builds in the necessary details to create for himself a father. For instance, in the home of Fred Halsey, he has described the portrait of an English gentleman—one who is cultured and seemingly wealthy. Toomer says that his nature and his features have been inherited by his great-grandson. Such is the picture that Toomer had always drawn of his paternal forebearers. In one of his biographies he has described his father as someone who resembled an Englishman—a man of distinction—and one who was not marked by black characteristics. Although Toomer never saw his father, these are the traits that he fondly imagines that he had. In the same room of Halsey's home, he pictures the portrait of a grandmother who has a Negro strain, possibly an explanation for his own Negro heritage.

Kabnis is a black neurotic who is described as having a lemon face, thin and silky hair and features generally associated with whites, all of which are features that Toomer possessed. Like Toomer, Kabnis has come South from the urbanized North to learn something about his roots and he finds what Toomer found in his own background, an agricultural setting. He is, like Toomer was, disillusioned at what he found in the South. He is made aware of the injustices heaped upon blacks by the whites of the South. He describes the deplorable cabins in which the blacks live and the domineering tones used in their voices when addressing blacks. All of these oppressive tactics are injustices which Toomer had not known before he went South. So with Kabnis.

Kabnis is a man who despairs easily and who calms himself with liquor and books. Toomer, likewise, was a man who despaired easily but who found his release in books. Toomer in other situations, such as his stay at the University of Wisconsin, at the City College of New York and at the University of Chicago, immersed himself in books and writing. Likewise, Kabnis is first shown as propped in bed reading, just as Toomer had pictured his Uncle Bismarck in one of his autobiographies. This picture of himself, surrounded by books and reading, constantly is one that pleased Toomer.

Again Toomer mirrored himself when he treats his ability to dance. In his autobiographies he has made no secret of the fact that he was a smooth dancer. In the first pages of "Kabnis," he describes how he goes through a grand march with Stella and how he grabs

Cora and parades around. It is now obvious that in seeing Kabnis we see Toomer. "Kabnis" is not the only work in which Toomer presents himself thinly disguised. For instance, in "York Beach," he is disguised as Nathan.

Cane's thematic circle has been completed with the return to the South. In Section One, Toomer presents the six primitive protagonists, all of whom live close to the soil. The lives of these six women, all highly sexed, serve to give an insight into southern life along the Dixie Pike. The second section of *Cane* takes place in Washington and in Chicago, where blacks who have retained an essence of their primitive ways live. These traits which they have retained from their more primitive ways are the characteristics which make their lives meaningful. The primitives who live close to the soil—to the cane and the harvest—and who are content to sleep and to love are the happiest. Blacks whose lives are confined by the social customs of the cities are in the process of losing their essential qualities for living. They have allowed themselves to become "dictie" and have hence lost their feeling for goodness and for brotherhood. In Washington, women have been confined by the customs of decorum, while men (like Rhobert, for instance, who allows house ownership to become an all-consuming passion) have emphasized material values so that they have lost insight into the beauty of life. The narrator views the "new black," the one who is moving rapidly into the confines of civilized society, with repulsion; the beauty lies with the fading "song-lit" race.

The final section of *Cane* treats of the tragic collapse of a young man who cannot adjust himself to an environment that will not allow him to enjoy the privileges of manhood and brotherhood and aesthetic beauty. Reared in the North where he had not lived under a daily fear of lynching, nor with a feeling of gross inferiority either to whites or to blacks who had achieved prominence because of their truculence to white ways, the protagonist slowly loses his sense of self-direction and lapses into self-hatred and indolence.

Robert Bone has said that a critical analysis of *Cane* is a frustrating task and that a process of restoration will destroy evidences of Toomer's art.[84]

It is true that *Cane* may, at first reading, seem artificial. In addition, Toomer's characters, for the most part, and especially those in Section One, are not substantial. Many of them are not fully developed and we gather only the very essences of their being. Karintha, for instance, remains a "whir" in the Georgia dusk. And we never see Fern clearly or know her fully; all we remember is that her "face flowed into her eyes," and that something which the narrator called God flows into her eyes.

If an analysis makes Toomer's early work seem incoherent, possibly a further look at his style will clarify some of the nebulous ideas conveyed by his work. Though "Kabnis" carries a more unified theme than some of the earlier pieces in *Cane*, the entire collection of short stories, poems, and sketches of the volume exemplifies Toomer's penetrating style. One of the dominant features of his style is the musical quality, notably in the first two parts of *Cane*. Frequently Toomer almost imperceptibly drifts from prose into poetry, and often his prose has a poetic ring to it. For instance, he says of Karintha, "She was as innocently lovely as a November cotton flower." Later he drifts from a musical passage into staccato phrases:

Karintha's running was a whir. It had the sound of the red dust that sometimes makes a spiral in the road. At dusk, during the hush after the sawmill had closed down, and before any of the women had started their supper-getting-ready songs, her voice, high-pitched, shrill, would put one's ears to itching. But no one ever thought to make her stop because of it. She stoned the cows, and beat her dog, and fought the other children.[85]

The sketch opens with a song in praise of Karintha, drifts into poetic prose, then into another song followed by snatches of description, and ends in a song. Little imagistic passages interspersing the narrative give rise to a vague portrait of Karintha: "Her skin is like dusk on the eastern horizon," "God grant us youth, secretly prayed the old men," "Karintha...was a wild flash," or she who carries beauty, "perfect as the dusk when the sun goes down."[86]

The word pictures of his characters are well-drawn even though he outlines his characters only by the faintest essences. Finally, however, the characters evolve from the sketchy narratives. Of this method, "Becky" is an excellent example, for we never see Becky, the protagonist, in reality. We come to know her only from the hearsay about her and from the unheard secret that the pines "whisper to Jesus." In "Becky" the matter-of-fact, straightforward language of the narrative is interspersed with clipped lines and singing phrases: "Becky was the white woman who had two Negro sons. She's dead; they've gone away."[87]

Frequently Toomer's narrator enters and interrupts the narrative to comment:

CHAPTER 3

The Veil Replaced

WITH the publication of *Cane* Toomer was recognized as a very promising young author. Among black authors, he was considered one of the best. His use of black materials as a basis for artistic creation had proved that black authors need not resort to sentimentalism or primitivism in order to create literature of merit out of materials at hand. Alain Locke, the noted literary historian whose field of specialization was black culture in the United States, included Toomer in his *New Negro* (1925) as one of the most gifted men of the Black Renaissance. Toomer's work was frequently anthologized in volumes of what was called black literature and he himself became a literary lion. In the black folk spirit, Toomer had found the emotional release which he sought. In *Cane*, he showed how many had lost their emotional spontaneity because of modern industrial society. He showed how blacks were victims of a bourgeois society which kept them so constrained that they were unable to find expression for their emotions. In fact, he developed a literary style that veered from that of black writers who were his contemporaries. Toomer went so far as to disassociate himself from racism. He had a creative imagination and he used this creative imagination with the materials that he found within the black race.

Jean Toomer was certainly well aware that his work had merit. Gorham Munson had told the young author that he had a capacity for producing great work and had listed Toomer, along with Hart Crane, as one of the most promising young writers in America. In 1929, Alfred Kreymborg had included Toomer as one of the finest authors "among the darker people." He says of him: "A philosopher and a psychologist by temperament, the Washington writer is now fascinated by the larger, rather than the parochial interests of the human race, and should some day compose a book in the grand manner."[1] But Toomer's attempts to transcend the "narrow parochial" of black literature, where he had initiated a fresh, new style of writing, were never realized. Though Toomer had at first been drawn to the life of primitive blacks and had utilized these materials for his work, his subsequent associations in literary circles with writers who were interested in all literature as art helped to convince him that his literary efforts ought not be confined to one racial or ethnic group. When, early in his literary career, Sherwood Anderson had commended him on his ability to write as a black, Toomer felt that he would, if he followed Anderson's suggestion, limit himself. He did not want to limit himself, nor did he want to be limited. His great concern for the development of his literary style is shown by this letter when he wrote to Waldo Frank:

He [Sherwood Anderson] limits me to Negro. As an approach, as a constant element (part of the larger whole) of interest, Negro is good. But to try to tie me to one of my parts is surely to lose me. My own letters have taken Negro as a point, and from there have circled out. Sherwood, for the most part, ignores the circles. In direct contact I am certain that I would like him. His notes have a full-hearted warmth and ease about them. But I need something more.[2]

Further evidence that he was not inclined to want to think, or even write, in terms solely "Negro" is evidenced by another statement in a letter to Frank:

The only time that I think "Negro" is when I want a peculiar emotion which is associated with this name. As a usual thing, I actually do not see differences of color and contour. I see differences of life and experience, and often enough these lead me to physical coverings. But not always, and from the standpoint of conventional criticism, not often enough. I'm very likely to be satisfied with a character whose body one knows nothing of.[3]

Toomer, as may well be seen by the above letter, did not want to limit himself to writing *about* blacks or *for* blacks. He wanted to "circle out," as he said, and write of the universal. Waldo Frank, his confidante and friend, agreed with Toomer that his greatest asset lay in his writing about life, not about any one race. He believed, like Toomer, that literature was not art unless it had universal significance. His reply to Toomer indicates that he agreed with him:

The day you write as a Negro, or an American, your work will lose a dimension. How typical that is of most recognition: that effort immediately to limit you, to put you in a cubbyhole and stick a label underneath. I intend, possibly above all else, in my introduction to *Cane* to point out that the important thing which has at length released you to creating is that you do not write as a Negro...that you take your race or your races naturally, as a white man takes his. The few talented writers among the Negroes have been ruined because they could not forget...the world would not let them...that they were Negroes. For an analogous reason, when the Jews were first liberated from the ghettos, they produced second-rate books and music and pictures; they were too conscious of the limiting detail of their race and consciousness of race became the norm of their creations, instead of consciousness of life itself. Precisely because you have been able to go South as a human being, among Negroes as one of them because you are a human being first, your work is released into real creation. And the miracle that came at me last fall with you, after several years of loving and understanding the South, was that I was also able to get to the deep reality in which color and race disappeared as entities: and took their place as mere surfaces. I am gratified that you reacted to S[herwood] A[nderson]'s response, flattering as it doubtless was, in the way you have. You are a strong deep man, my brother, and I not only love you: I am proud of you.— I was moved to send you a wire to give you an idea of the HURRAH of your letter (and the relief,) it gave me.[4]

At this point, just at the time that he had developed the convictions that race and color ought to be considered as "mere surfaces" in the utilization of materials for creative art, other of his associations became decisive factors in Toomer's life. These associations, which developed as the result of his literary accomplishments and of his personal life, were to influence his entire literary career profoundly.

Jean Toomer's involvement with the problems of "writing Negro" and that of his own racial identity may now be called the key to the mystery that has seemingly surrounded his life. In *Black and White*, David Littlejohn in his assessment of recent literature by American Negroes says of Toomer:

Jean Toomer's career is still wrapped in foggy mystery: he wrote one esoteric work, difficult to grasp, define, and assess; he was associated with one of the more advanced white modernist cults, and adopted and taught Russian mysticism; and then he suddenly declared himself white, and disappeared.[5]

Jean Toomer's career is no longer wrapped in "foggy mystery," nor did he disappear. The "mystery" of Toomer's life was cleared up when Fisk University recently obtained his private correspondence and the manuscripts of his unpublished novels, plays, criticism, poetry, and short stories. A careful study of these papers will show that Toomer's work after 1930 was greatly influenced by certain of his beliefs, which may be clarified if we review some of his works concerning the position of the black and of other races in America. Toomer's papers show that Toomer continued writing, always hopeful that one of his longer works would be accepted for publication, until a few years before his death on March 30, 1967.

Littlejohn also says that Toomer "declared himself white." Toomer did not declare himself white, but he did refuse to be placed in any one racial category in America and to have his literary work assessed by standards reserved for black literature. By refusing to "write Negro," by refusing to identify with any race other than the American race, and by refusing permission for his work to be published in volumes of "Negro literature," Toomer hoped to escape having his work judged by standards other than those which apply to all American literature.

Let us here revert for a moment to the publicity which Toomer received following his best-known work, *Cane*, in order that we may see the course of events which caused him to assume the position that he was not of the black race, but of the American race. *Cane* was called the "best book ever written by a Negro author," but it sold fewer than a thousand copies. Reasons for the limited circulation are obvious. Blacks of the 1920s felt that Toomer had betrayed his race by writing frankly about sexual deviation among the primitives of their race and among the so-called "dictie" blacks. Furthermore, white audiences were little interested in "Negro literature" (either that by or about blacks) that digressed from the usual plantation or sensational traditions. Moreover, the number of educated blacks who had either the money to buy or the inclination to read such works as Toomer's were few in number. Toomer's problem with his writing then became a racial problem in more ways than one. During the Twenties, for instance, when Toomer was engaged in his most active public literary work, relations between the two races were not carried on with the freedom that they are today. Segregation was practiced in the North almost as rigidly as in the South. Even in Harlem, at the famous Cotton Club and the Savoy, where the whites came in large numbers to learn about black music, art, and culture, blacks were frequently not admitted. But Toomer himself was what is sometimes called a "voluntary Negro" and he associated freely in both white and black society. He became race conscious in that he firmly believed that race existed only on the surface. In fact, after his affiliation with the Gurdjieff movement which sent him first to France and then to Chicago and Portage, Wisconsin, where he set up classes of interested enthusiasts, Toomer, more often than not, associated with literary and social groups that were mainly nonblack. For instance, the literary coterie formed by him, Hart Crane, Waldo Frank, and Gorham Munson after they became obsessed with the theories of Ouspensky was one of his most important associations. In addition, his voluminous correspondence shows that his friends, both men and women, accepted him for what he was, an intelligent young author who was a skillful literary craftsman. In 1930, he conducted a series of lectures in Chicago on "The Psychology and Craft of Writing," and frequently the newspaper notices of his lectures, as well as reviews of his privately printed volume of aphorisms called *Essentials* (1931), failed to indicate that Toomer was the author of the volume of black folk realism entitled *Cane*, although his work which appeared in *Dial*, the *Little Review, Pagany, Broom,* and other small magazines was often listed. His Chicago associations and his experiments with the Gurdjieff movement in Wisconsin resulted in his marriage to Margery Bodine Latimer, the author of several novels and a protege of Zona Gale and Joseph Hergesheimer. A few months later nationwide attention was attracted to this marriage when a *Time* reporter interviewed the couple at an artists' colony in Carmel, California.[6] When it was revealed that Toomer had been at one time identified as a black, unfavorable publicity developed because of the interracial marriage. From that time on, Toomer ceased to write aesthetically of blacks. He began to confine his writing to materials outside the black race itself and to consider himself a member of, as he said, the American race. He made this statement:

Americans probably do not realize it,...but there are no racial barriers anymore, because there are so many Americans with strains of Negro, Indian, and Oriental blood. As I see America, it is like a great stomach into which are thrown the elements which make up the life blood. From this source is coming a distinct race of people. They will achieve tremendous works of art, literature and music. They will not be white, black, or yellow—just American.[7]

Even before the unfavorable national publicity following the marriage to Margery Latimer, Toomer had been deeeply concerned with the "hypnotic division of Americans into black and white." He was concerned that this "hypnotic division" had affected art and literature; yet Toomer himself became the victim of the hypnosis that had such a great hold on American society. After the publication of *Cane*, he made no further attempts to establish any kinship with his racial past as had been the purpose of his trip to Georgia, which had produced *Cane*.

In 1932, after Miss Nancy Cunard, a French woman interested in compiling a volume of "documentary facts on Africa and the question of color in the U.S.A. and Europe," had asked him to make a contribution to her volume, Toomer replied to her:

Your article "Black Man and White Ladyship," together with the announcement and your note to me, reached me in California. Your paper is a very interesting piece of work. And the forthcoming book promises much. Since the publication of my book "Cane" there have unfortunately arisen certain misunderstandings as to myself and my position. Though I am interested in and deeply value the Negro, I am not a Negro. And though I have written about the Negro, and value the material and the art that is Negro, all of my writings during the past seven years have been on other subjects. In America I am working for vision of this country as composed of people who are Americans first, and only of certain descents as secondary matters. In order to establish my view I have had—for a time—to swing into a rather extreme position which has not allowed me to be associated with any race other than what we may call the American race. This will explain why I cannot respond in the matter of collaborating with you in your new book. I am sorry. And I appreciate your writing to me.[8]

There was, as Toomer himself indicates in this letter to Miss Cunard, a drastic change in the style of his writing. This change in style developed over a period of years and may be attributed to the social factors in Toomer's life that seemingly necessitated a statement of his racial position. In addition to having refused Miss Cunard's request, Toomer also refused to have his work included in James Weldon Johnson's *The Book of American Negro Poetry* or to send a copy of *Essentials* to the Schomberg Collection of Negro Literature of the New York Public Library.[9] As S. P. Fullinwider says: "The story of Toomer's literary efforts after 1923 is a story of frustration, despair, and failure.... Toomer's story is one of a young man caught up in the tangled skein of race relations in America."[10] And so he was.

The letter to Miss Cunard represents a tremendous modification of Jean Toomer's position toward the black. Only ten years after he had made a pilgrimage to Georgia so that he might listen to those of his own racial roots "caroling softly souls of slavery," Toomer had begun to swing, as he said, into an extreme position and to consider himself a member of the "American race." He lost his interest in seeking his identity with and in seeking out the beauty of the black race.

We know that Toomer had certainly felt a close bond with blacks early in his literary career. His ability to treat black characters with sympathy and understanding is evidenced by *Cane*, and especially in the dramatic novella "Kabnis" in which, as has been previously noted, he depicted a young nearly white black who could not come to grips with his ancestral heritge nor his penchant for literary expression. Further concrete evidence of his early concern of Toomer may be seen in his unpublished essay "The Negro Emergent," which outlines the sociological forces which at the time of its writing (about 1925) had long held blacks suppressed.[11] In this essay Toomer reviews the factors which have kept the blacks from emerging and recognizing their inner being. The constant process of self-discovery has been difficult for the black in America because of the "crust" that has been forced upon him by external circumstances —circumstances which have been created by the dominant white world. The black is, he says, divorced from his racial roots for two reasons. He wants to, first of all, force all thoughts of his slave roots from his mind because of the concept of inferiority that has been associated with these roots. Then, too, the American black, who is frequently a product of African and white civilizations, is cut off from his white roots which set him apart and deny him. Because blacks have been used as slave laborers and as concubines, they have been made to feel inferior. Not only has this inferiority been developed by whites toward blacks, says Toomer, but blacks have (at the encouragement of the whites) developed social and economic preferences among themselves because of skin color.

During the time of the writing of this essay, Toomer notes that the blacks of America are beginning to emerge from the status imposed upon them by whites. They are beginning to hear the beauty in their spirituals. They are, in addition, beginning to love the soil which they had been made to hate because they were forced to face it. Now that the black is recognizing his roots in his racial past, he is uncovering his soul. Toomer says of the status of the black as he is emerging to the creative level in America:

The Negro is led through himself outward to the surrounding world. He feels his own milieu to be desirable: its beauty, ugliness, passion, poverty, rhythm, and color. There is truth in the statement that Harlem differs from other communities in shade merely, but not in pattern. But it should be remembered that this shade appeals to something more than the eye of a Negro. He wishes to generously partake of it; he wishes to press beyond its boundaries, for he knows that neither his nor any similar group provides the range to satisfy a large capacity and keen appetite for experience. He is frank to recognize the advanced status of the white creative world in the matters of discovery and experiment. He wishes to learn from it. But now he does not meet it as a white world, for he recognizes there his own impulses, gone farther, more matured. He meets it as a world of similar values. While he is uncovering the life of Harlem, he is exploring New York. While he finds out things about himself, he learns what other men have found out of themselves. In short, he is emerging to the creative level of America.

But more rapidly than he emerges towards it, the white world of America steps towards him. The Negro is being studied in relation to the general economic problems. The problems of population. He challenges attention from those who are sincere in their democracy. His social and educational aspects are being investigated and aided. Psychoanalysis has interesting data concerning him. Articles about him are appearing with increasing frequency in the leading magazines and newspapers. Books are coming out, and publishers are receptive of Negro material. Clubs, societies, and forums wish to hear about the Negro. All this is indicative of a certain type of discovery. I had in mind particularly, however, the discovery of the Negro by creative America.[12]

The discovery of himself will have profound effects on the black man who is emerging, Toomer concludes.

Discovery implies receptivity to all things; the rejection of no single one, save it be unreal. Prior to the present phase, because he was denied by others the Negro denied them and necessarily denied himself. Forced to say nay to the white world, he was negative toward his own life. Judged by appearance, he considered appearances seriously, and had no time to find out what lay beneath the creature that America had made of him. And since he rejected this creature, he rejected everything. Something has happened. I have tried to suggest the nature of this happening. An impulse is at work within him, transforming rejections to acceptances, denials to affirmations. It is detaching the essential Negro from the social crust. One may define the impulse; it would be premature to name the substances that may be revealed by it. I think it best not to attempt it. For should there be set up an arbitrary figure of a Negro, composed of what another would have him like, and the assertion made that he should model himself after it, this figure, though prompted by the highest interest, would nevertheless share the false and constricting nature of all superimposed images. Rather, I would be receptive of his reality as it emerges (being active only by way of aid to this emergence), assured that in proportion as he discovers what is real within him, he will create, and by that act at once create himself and contribute his value to America.[13]

"The Negro Emergent," alludes to some of the problems which confronted the protagonists of *Cane*. Many of these protagonists, especially those of the Washington and Chicago scenes, denied their past. Only when they came to recognize the roots of their racial past were they able to come to grips with their status as blacks. On the contrary, only those protagonists such as Karintha, who lived close to the soil, felt the beauty and the "whir" of life.

In this essay, Toomer's closeness to the race is clearly defined. He recognizes the psychological problems that face the black of the 1920s and the social climate in which he was forced to live. He is aware that the "external circumstances" of the black's life have forced him away from his racial roots. The Jean Toomer who wrote of this black life had likewise been divorced from his roots and he was familiar with "anemia and chronic invalidism" that could develop.

Toomer, as time passed, became less outspoken on issues as they related specifically to the black. His interest in the black became less personal and his views broadened to that of racial problems in general. Early in the Twenties, he had held strongly to the idea that the black had not clung strongly enough to the Southern folk-spirit. In that spirit, as was shown in "Box Seat," says Toomer, blacks could find emotional release, rather than follow in blind adulation the overcivilized blacks who were aping white society. With such blacks as those of rural Georgia where he had visited, Toomer felt— and tried to develop—a kinship.

By 1928, however, Toomer was facing the black and his problems differently. A lengthy discussion of his views of the problems of the racial crisis, such as that in America, is contained in his essay, "Race Problems and Modern Society," in *Problems of Civilization*, edited by Baker Brownell of Northwestern University. Toomer, at the time of publication of this article, had been enjoying popularity as a philosopher and lecturer in Chicago, and his opinions were esteemed by many critics. In this essay, Toomer views the problem of race in America, not as a black, but as one who looks at the whole issue objectively. Taking the United States as a sufficiently representative example of modern society, he sees the causes of what is termed race prejudice as economic and political. He maintains that the term "race," rather than applying to a "clearly delimitable, homogeneous biological group," is rather a social classification, and a confused and uncertain subject. "A race, it turns out, is a group of people that we treat as if they were one. You belong to a certain race, if you feel yourself to be a member, and if others treat you as if you were."[14] He further states that race is a matter of public opinion, and not a question that can be easily settled by science, and that race problems are actually psychological and sociological in cause and in character. Toomer contends that both blacks and whites are drawing lines between their own cultures and are, at the same time, following cultural patterns that "make the drawing of distinctions supposedly based on skin color or blood composition" more and more ridiculous. He concludes by saying that the solution of race problems can never be effected until there is a "fusion of racial and cultural factors in America, in order that the best possible stock and culture may be produced."[15]

Toomer was developing democratic ideas about the existence of races in America. He had already begun to see that his work was being judged as well as being rejected on the basis of race and he therefore decided to devote his literary talents to an autobiography or perhaps a novel to promote an idea which he hoped would dissolve some of America's racial lines of demarcation. Waldo Frank had told Toomer that he did not write "as a Negro," but that he accepted his races naturally, just as any other American. This is precisely the manner in which Toomer had wanted to write—as an artist, not as a black artist. Toomer had said in 1931 in *Essentials*, "I am of no race. I am of the human race."[16] He reaffirmed this position later in a letter concerning the inclusion of his work in the category of "Negro literature":

I am of the human race, a man at large in the human world, preparing a new race. This is an accurate statement of my position as it regards race. I am disassociating my name and self from racial classifications, as I believe that the real values of life necessitate it. This is my stand not only for myself, but for all Americans and for people in general.[17]

This concept, that all races of America have been fused into one race, is the ultimate position that Toomer assumed and to which he devoted his final literary efforts.

CHAPTER 4

Uncollected Works

JEAN Toomer never again achieved the artistic recognition aroused by the publication of *Cane*. He began to experiment more with creative material which would meld his growing philosophic interest with his writing. From our perspective, this trend proved to be an artistic misstep since the more Toomer became involved with his "new" writing, the wider the gap he created between himself and his audience. This difficult period was not without its highlights and successful periods of writing, however, and Toomer did create at a regular and significant rate. The basic problem of Toomer's audience—that of attempting to interpret and comprehend precisely what he was about—was largely overcome by the brilliance of *Cane*. This is not the case with the bulk of the material Jean Toomer wrote, published and unpublished, after 1923. Nearly all this material remains neglected and unavailable to the general reader. The purpose of this section is to discuss four representative works from the period following *Cane* in order to gauge the distance or merit of these later works. These works include the short stories "Easter," "Winter on Earth," "Mr. Costyve Duditch," and the poem "Blue Meridian."

I *"Easter"*

"Easter" is an uncollected five-page sketch published in the *Dial* in 1925. Since it is one of the first important pieces published after *Cane*, "Easter" represents the initiation of a new literary direction for Toomer. It is, therefore, a hallmark in Toomer's canon. Michael Krasney notes that "with the publication of this sketch, he abandoned black materials for literary art, *Cane*'s impressionistic realism, and the expressionism of the earlier drama."[1] If readers and critics alike had some difficulty understanding *Cane*, they were undoubtedly baffled by the material presented in "Easter." It has no plot, only a few indistinctly outlined characters, is seemingly unconnected, and seems to abandon art for artifice.

"Easter" begins with Toomer's description of a scene in the manner of an observer verbalizing a painting which contains many divergent scenes. People are waiting for resurrection from their own sterility. this anticipation is directly related to the subconscious impact of longing for Christ's return to earth. This belief persists throughout the entire Christian world and is a causative factor in how one reacts to a personal, individualized, spiritual crisis. Six hundred sixty-six people are involved in this scene. They converse "as if in effort to avert catastrophe. It sounded like flies buzzing in a monkey house."[2] After some length of time, many hours, four hundred and sixty-six leave and "there remained two hundred." These two hundred discuss varied topics but "their words, strings, that wound fat balls about the subjects. The balls were set up like ten-pins and bowled over."[3] These conversations consist of almost pure rhetoric. The hubbub is interrupted when a bootlegger rises and makes a plea. He wants to use his wealth for a liberal education since "his money had come easy, it had come dangerously."[4] One person is delegated to offer the bootlegger individual instruction in l'Histoire des Mangols-de in Djami-el-Ternuik de Fadl Allah Rashid et-Din. Shortly thereafter, one hundred and ninety-four persons "beat it," leaving a remainder of six people.

Of those who depart, three are examined in detail. The first is a woman who cannot find her house because she is dizzy and they all look the same to her. A policeman offers her assistance. He tells her to jump on her house as it goes spinning by. She does so, landing in a darkened room containing the expression "Give up or get out." She is trapped in a bawdy house, choosing to give up any attempt to change herself.[5]

The second is a preacher who proceeds to Bethlehem where he posts the following proclamation:

We are coming toward Holy Week, and unless we can come together at the Cross, unless we are one in Christ, we are not Christians, and this step toward the unification of the Methodist Church North and the Methodist Church South is a step toward making all one in Christ.[6]

This crusade is spiritual and personal but Toomer undercuts its religious significance by emphasizing church politics.

The third is an excited young boy who races to 125th and 7th Avenues. Three corners are occupied by the Mormons, the Salvation Army, and a soap-box orator speaking on behalf of liberty bonds. The youth takes possession of the fourth corner, proclaiming "We are come to that place where the mollusk's praise is magnificent; but where huge cries become inaudible before they reach the eardrums."[7] It would appear that the youth is appealing for more humanity for the masses.

Several others of those who fled are noted, bringing the total to fourteen. Toomer inserts descriptions of thoughts by a laborer, an infant, a philosopher, a psychologist, and a poet among others. Each description contains some general relationship to a search for inner peace, a serenity none is able to achieve. The last individual described is a woman, in heavy labor, who asks an old man to call her a taxi. The man dies while she is on her way to the hospital. She gives birth to a boy who "amazed everyone by ordering his mother out of bed to run an errand for him."[8] This anachronistic development has religious overtones. Could it be that the old man is reincarnated into the body of the child? A better word might be "resurrected" because in the paragraphs which immediately follow the six who had remained in the house await Easter. It is April 3 and the waiting has become unbearable. Suddenly, the earth splits and "he" arises into their midst. The group flees, leaving him alone in the house.

He begins a sermon thus: "Thou, immeasurable source and boundary—" but loses himself in thought. He cannot reorder his thoughts and resorts to a memorized quote which allows him to continue his speech: "Let God be given as the cause of all, himself uncaused, uncreated, and unborn."[9] As he contemplates the meaning of such statements, his mind again wanders. Six hundred sixty-six thoughts beset him, among which are elements of the preceding categories of people who occupied the house originally. His last thought is of the preacher who journeyed to Bethlehem to post the proclamation.

The selection ends so abruptly that one is taken by surprise. Toomer implies that religion, especially religion based on a savior who will return to earth and rescue the true believer, is in the mind of the believer. It is an answer but not an ultimate inviolate one. "Easter" is a powerful and emotional piece and a successful experiment with form.

II *"Winter on Earth"*

"Winter on Earth" was published in *The Second American Caravan: A Yearbook of American Literature* in 1928. It was edited by the distinguished trio, Alfred Kreymborg, Lewis Mumford, and Paul Rosenfeld. The collection was, indeed, a notable one and represented much of the finest writing of the period. Other authors whose selections were included in *The Second American Caravan* were Sherwood Anderson, Robert Penn Warren, Robert Frost, and Katherine Anne Porter, among many others. The biographical sketch in "Notes on Contributors" which Toomer submitted is revealing. It reads:

> Jean Toomer was born in Washington, D.C. on December 26, 1894. He studied in the University of Wisconsin, and the College of the City of New York. He is the author of *Cane*, and *The Gallonwerps* and is a contributor to the *New World Series*, edited by Baker Brownell. He has published in the *Double Dealer, Broom,* and the *Dial.*[10]

Toomer implies that he had published significant works beyond *Cane*. He had not. The fact that he was published in this volume is reason enough to give "Winter on Earth" a close reading. Moreover, it is a work distinguished by its uniqueness in Toomer's canon. Toomer was attempting to shift his fictive stance from the emotional strains so evident in *Cane* to the more objective rendering of his prose. This stance emerged from his Gurdjiefian influence and hailed a new kind of writing from Toomer, even more radical than his preceding experimentations. "Winter on Earth" is fundamentally sound and a work of minor importance but it must have confused and even shocked readers who expected material similar to that engendered by *Cane*.

"Winter on Earth" is a narrative which, on the surface at least, is consistent only in its inconsistencies. The analysis of the narrative thrust which follows provides substantial proof of this point since, as each segment is noted, the threads of plot spiral outward, incomplete and provocative.

Consisting of seven sections, "Winter on Earth" begins with an aphoristic opening section concerned with spatial and temporal interpretations of time. Repetition of key verbs provides a tonal and grammatical sense of unity to the first paragraph. The words "recur," "start," "stop," and "see" initiate this unity. There is also an attempt to delineate the segments of time which one can actually experience including the seasons in the first paragraph, days in the second, and minutes in the third. The section ends with an aphoristic interrogative further qualifying man's sense of self as he measures himself in relation to time. Toomer asks, "What significance does a man derive from his existence?" The question is intended to be taken as an initial step toward a new sense of awareness. Only by constant scrutiny and self-evaluation can mankind hope to achieve insight.

Section Two, four times the length of Section One, begins with a further qualification. The subject is knowledge coupling itself with the significance question. Earth time is reckoned by the way men "see" Earth's calendar. It is all a matter of perspective. To the ancient, the physical earth appears young; to the young, it appears ancient. America is merely a geographical base for ideas and people. Toomer again employs the Whitmanesque technique of self-contradictory statements here by stating, "No more. No less," and then, "Ah, yes, much more, much less."

The next several paragraphs in Section Two further undermine the broad delineation of time in man's life since Toomer assumes that there was time when there were no seasons interspersed with a single sentence paragraph resembling an aphorism from *Essentials*. After noting the relationship of history to time, he inserts a series of staccato interrogatories.

"To what purpose? Why are there seasons? Why is the moon? Why is there time for things to happen in? Why are there men? Why are there eyes? Why do they see? Why do they not see?"[11]

Americans, relatively untouched by natural disaster, equate the passage of time, or rather the lack of it, with historical events, thus weakening their proximity to the rhythms of nature. This deteriorating position is emphasized for the remainder of Section Two, again by the use of a series of interrogatories culminating in "What purpose do they find in sleep?...We sleep. Who profits by our dreams?"[12]

Section Three initiates a more concrete narrative thrust in "Winter on Earth." It is winter and the season is furiously evident. Everywhere the cold becomes an overriding concern. Two young men, dressed only in thin coats, stumble across the blank, silent landscape, shivering and muttering about the intensity of nature's wrath. They curse the cold, humanity, and finally, the earth itself. One asks, "Who the hell fixed this earth?" The other replies, "Go south." "But south is no better," retorts his companion. One would roast there and if he didn't believe it, why did his friend not stay in the South? The omnipresent cold brings terror to those exposed to the elements. "The cold made men everywhere begrudge their energies." Then the snow returns to further agitate and terrify the inhabitants of earth in winter. Toomer assumes a pragmatic style and tone here. He compares and contrasts the destiny of randomly falling snowflakes to the random, unknowing and oftentimes indifferent posture of men whose destiny it is to also ride the winds of chance. "The white snow was heedless of the terror men would feel where they crystallized in space far above the earth and made to whirl and fall upon an unknown surface."[13] Just as men wander aimlessly in the snowstorm, individuals who have lost their sense of place, a reference point to discern the meanings of their existence, are doomed to empty, unproductive lives. This particular sequence is remarkably attuned to the visual image being presented since carefully composed lyric sentences are interspersed at random in the section, coinciding with the image of snowflakes as they glitter among the barren landscape, randomly reflecting light and falling to the earth intermittently. "Blast of wind swept over the bleak hill and whistled and mourned when anything resisted them," and "the moon glowed in a black sky like a disc of silver" are such examples which glitter amongst the dreary descriptions of the reaction the two young men have to the overwhelming winter forces. The intent is to develop a frame of reference for the reader, a framework which is so apparently lacking in the humanity facing nature. Toomer begins to prepare the reader for an anslysis of the distinction between mere existence and a life with meaning and some directed purpose.

Placed in the center of this section is a vignette entitled "The Young Man Who Tripped On." The title character represents a marked contrast to the preceding young men dressed so poorly against the weather. He is in a jovial mood, in opposition to their hostility. This young man emerges into the streets after an all-night party. A pastiche concerning the party itself reveals a highly charged sexual situation where trysts between licit and illicit couples take place. As he walks, i.e., trips, gloating over his recent conquest of his friend's wife, he suddenly melds with the world around him, losing the personal facts embedded in his memory which gives him distinctions of individuality.

His name, his occupation, his place of residence, the make of his car, what kind of clothes he wore, the number of his insurance policy, even his telephone number, in fact, all phone numbers and everything just suddenly passed away from him as though they had never been.[14]

Evidently, Toomer means for the reader to connect this development to his concept of universal memory, so evident in his canon. It also connects the young man's plight to the matter of perspective outlined in the opening sections of "Winter on Earth." It would probably stretch a point to connect the literal *Cane* that the young man carries to *Cane* itself but the epigrammatic concluding simile repeated from the earlier portion of this section, "the moon glowed in a black sky like a disc of silver," is certainly akin to the lyricisms of that volume.

In the next several pages, "Winter on Earth" projects a camera eye, at once focusing close-up of men and women encountering the snow and cold in the streets and then presenting filtered, fragmented but panoramic descriptions of the entire street scene. Some profit by and some curse the snow—the important point is that no one is indifferent to it. Chicago is snowbound and its inhabitants are forced to run in place, paralyzed by the wrath and incredible beauty of nature. One man curses the snow because it will prevent him from closing a lucrative business transaction. Another recalls his first kiss with a lost love "who had ever since consistently refused to marry him." One old woman with insomnia is reminded of quarrels with relations of her married children. She believes that her death is imminent and comforts herself by reading about Christ's birth. Two others, Harry and his girlfriend, remind each other that going through life alone is difficult. She believes the snow a romantic setting, enhancing their intimacy. Harry finds the snow a nuisance. Abruptly, he decides to go home before it's too late to catch a train. Harry is a realist. Toomer summarizes the effect on these individuals with "Before daylight, in different places, a number of men-children were born upon the earth. And these were those who made swift transits, which men call death, into either nothing or into an unimaginable world."[15]

The remainder of Section Three is taken up with Toomer's rather obtuse discussion of meaning when it is distorted by convention. There is little intimate conversation and basic humanity even in a natural setting. The last paragraph brilliantly summarizes the heretofore unapparent connection between human communication and a winter storm and localized personal self-knowledge which rightfully should become a portion of the universal family of man.

But while it snowed, some force of nature thawed men out and allowed them to feel just a little bit that, after all, they were all in the world together. Doubtless some men took advantage of this good feeling. But there was enough of it to survive these shocks, so that even conductors had a few good words for the crowds that jammed and jostled in streetcars. Automobiles got stuck in ruts of snow. Other cars, instead of honking their heads off with irritation and impatience, honked and sounded for the fun of it, gave the stuck cars boosts, and helped them get started. Men gave their arms to women over crossings. And there was occasional camaraderie, gaiety, and laughter as men and women, all bundled up, trudged and crunched back and forth along the snow-packed sidewalks.

Section Four abruptly changes setting and tone, becoming an island. The island includes a legendary "Lover's Leap." The rock itself is the site of a friendly spot amongst the bleakness of the landscape and the loveliness of the island's inhabitants. But, instead of thematically developing the isolation element of Section Three and its obvious relation to the island, Toomer proceeds to inform the reader that this island, White Island, is indeed more of a paradise than it would first appear. On the summit of White Island is a stone structure, a house of God, again clouded in legend. It is architecturally perfect and serves as a link to the Island's anestral chain. Toomer filigrees his portrait of the island by connecting the Lover's Leap and the house of God by revealing the fact that all paths originate and terminate at some surprising spot. The sea makes its presence felt as much as the snow in Chicago but it appears far more benevolent.

Instead of being totally isolated, the inhabitants of White Island have traversed the globe, only to return seeking the solace of this gift from nature. Toomer states, "to be from White Island was to have a universal passport," one reason being that "stranger" also means "guest" in their language. Any visitor became caught up in the friendly, festive singing, a traditional method of celebration. Even more impressive to visitors is the successful unification of purpose by the islanders. It is a communal life style with each individual contributing his talents, and each leader or governor stepping forth as the situation arises rather than being elected.

Several instances of a White Islander's development are included here, one an apparent reference to Toomer's own experiences but emphasis is placed on another islander, Jend, who journeyed to the Orient. His arrival home, after twenty years, is eagerly anticipated. Jend is remembered as an extraordinarily gifted youth, almost the ultimate in human perfection. This acknowledgment coincides with Toomer's recounting of the entire legend of White Island. It was thought to have been settled by angels sent from God, commissioned to renew a sense of universal harmony. The island itself was chosen because it was isolated and "washed with clean waters." A man-child was supposedly washed ashore on the golden sand as an angel observed. He was subsequently reared to manhood and marriage to a young angel, beginning the race of White Islanders, also called the Children of the Sun.

Toomer concludes the legend noting that Naril, a beautiful young woman, anxiously awaits the return of Jend, her Jend. The section concludes with a brief paragraph describing a prairie blizzard and a series of enigmatic phrases ending with "I walk through the Universe."

Section Five presents yet another facet of Toomer's analysis of man's relationship to himself and the universe. Here two men are walking in the shadow of a great cathedral, an image juxtaposed against the majestic spirituality of the house of God in Section Four. One of these men resembles the approximate perfection of Jend. Although considerably older, "knowledge, love, and power—these attributes in him—were perfectly formed and blended in supreme synthesis."[16] The other man, thirty and confused, is a pupil deeply aware of his own human failings. The wise one states,

Provided that you make effort, you will gradually learn what and why you and all men are. But now you must acquire an essential sense of where you are and all men are. Men are in the Universe. Without the world-view which arises from this sense of actual location, which is the sense of actual existence, you will not be able to go far.[17]

Again, Toomer stresses the motif of location as an index to understanding. It is clearly his most concrete statement on the thematic thrust of the narrative.

The wise one continues by stating that the first step to self-mastery is to become "master in power, love, and knowledge" of oneself. As the two mutual friends part for some duration, a deeply moving aura of love overcomes the younger. He is blessed and quickly left to his own thoughts. The elder's work on earth is finished and he prepared to return "to the Unknown Father, the Prime Source, the great darkness, immovable, more luminous than light."[18] The section concludes on a note of contemplative peace and comparative solitude.

Section Six begins with the previous location motif, "Wherever men go, whatever they do, they are in the Universe." Whitmanesque categorizing and classification reinforce the concept of Universals. Characteristically, Toomer exclaims a barbaric yelp of his own as he exhorts the reader to realize that he cannot escape the Universe and Him, a deeply religious admonition.

Section Seven, an epilogue of sorts, consists of a series of interrogatories, all beginning with "Have you ever been solitary and exposed in a wilderness of unbroken...desert, ocean, Earth, and...Universe."[19] Toomer has taken the reader over the long route from the desert of Chicago, the White Island, the family of men, all housed in the universe whose architect is God.

The last paragraph is enigmatic, presenting a monologue addressed to a loved one, summarizing the lessons inculcated during the course of "Winter on Earth." It seems as if Toomer is bitter in this admonition of the reader. He offers the friendliness of a human heart but undercuts his presentation. One is now "powerfully alone" and the sense of isolation leaves the reader totally without a sense of catharsis in "Winter on Earth."

The best single study of "Winter on Earth" is found in Michael Krasney's analysis of Toomer's philosophic influences. Krasney approaches the narrative almost exclusively through the Gurdjieff philosophy, applying its methodology to the scope, format, and interpretation of "Winter on Earth." Krasney correctly notes

...the seven sections of "Winter on Earth" correspond to Gurdjieff's fundamental cosmological principle, the Law of Seven or the Law of the Octave, symbolically represented by the circumference of a circle—the enneagram. The enneagram functions in a manner similar to the tonal musical scale (or the days of the week); that is, whether viewed ascendingly or descendingly, the Law of Seven operates in a chain of eternal recurrence or eternal repetition, correspondingly working in harmony with the Law of Three.

The Gurdjieff cosmology is constructed to encircle the expanses of a macrocosm. The macrocosm is harmonious and can best be described as the living organism of the universe. Man functions within the concentric design. The outermost circle, that in which most men live, is the circle of tongues, tantamount to a state of sleep which men presume to be their waking state. The circles progress inwardly from the circle of tongues (confusion) to, next, the esoteric circle (regular or clear consciousness), then the mesoteric circle (self-remembering), and finally, to the innermost circle of the esoteric (objective consciousness where unity, being, and will are one). "Winter on

Earth" is a paradigm designed to render objectively the esoteric conception of the Law of Seven and to demonstrate its relationship to the four circles.[20]

Krasney's concise summary of the relationship between the Gurdjieff philosophy and Toomer's structural method in "Winter on Earth" helps to explain several difficulties with an analysis of the narrative. It is not an autobiographical study of Toomer's loss of creativity nor is it a dull, repetitive, and generally unconneced recapitulation of Toomer's theme of sterility in modern life so well expressed in "Rhobert," "Theatre," and "Kabnis" in *Cane*. Rather, it is something altogether new. Toomer exhibited a great deal of courage as experimentalist here, an acknowledgment which is long overdue. "Winter on Earth" remains a readable and thought-provoking piece.

III *"Mr. Costyve Duditch"*

"Mr. Costyve Duditch," a companion story to "Winter on Earth," is an enigmatic and experimental narrative. It was published in the *Dial* in December 1928[21] and remains an uncollected selection. "Mr. Costyve Duditch" is a finely drawn pencil portrait of one Costyve Duditch, an eccentric of the first order. The narrative is related in the third person, with point of view shifting from omniscient narrator to the two principal characters, Duditch himself and J. Breastbuck Coleeb. The elements of shifting perspectives and point of view are the most obvious experimental elements in "Mr. Costyve Duditch" and they bear some relationship to the analysis of Toomer's intent for the narrative. Such an explanation follows a brief summary of the plot. Apparently, Toomer means for the reader to adopt a "Miniver Cheevy" stance toward his title character. Both Cheevy and Duditch are out of step with so-called real time. Each appears to be more comfortable in the past. This acknowledgment is probably the key to any interpretation of "Mr. Costyve Duditch." Toomer develops the characterization of Duditch from time lapse frames. Duditch apparently has success-fully made the transition between the nebulous, fragmented world he traverses and the concrete, rigidly assigned world of conventional life, a world which he enters at his whim.

The narrative begins in Chicago, during one of its characteris-tically blustery days. The first individual we encounter is one Mr. J.

Breastbuck Coleeb, a person the narrator describes as "a man in the early forties, well trained in the natural sciences and a rather keen observer of human conduct."[22] In the midst of this particular observation, Coleeb undergoes an epiphany of sorts, concluding that he and his fellow creatures are bullied by the winds and that "he, a human intelligence, in this trivial circumstance, was giving sufficient evidence of man's helplessness in nature."[23] Coleeb's next observation is far less philosophical; rather, it depends on a sartorial comment. He sees a man rapidly approaching in a velour hat and a rather smart morning suit. It is Costyve Duditch who passes by, impervious to the wind or any pedestrian he might know. Coleeb manages to hail down this strange man and is greeted with the most hearty of handshakes. Duditch is in Chicago for only a day or so. It is only a stopover in his journeys. Duditch is, in fact, a world traveller, picking his itinerary in the most random fashions. Since their last meeting, Duditch has been in Spain, Constantinople, Persia, and Peking. Coleeb notes that various acquaintances have been wondering about the whereabouts of Duditch which pleases him enormously. Duditch replies, "Conceive it!"

Apparently, Duditch is touchy about the subject of his travels, preferring one to assume that he has far more roots than he, in truth, has. Noticing the sensitivity, Coleeb says, "You shy from what you fear may be criticisms of your wandering? You feel they think you are a sort of aimless globetrotter, the proverbial rolling stone which gathers no moss?"[24] Indeed, Coleeb proceeds to rebut the value judgments of such people as Duditch argues against rootlessness. Toomer implies here that Duditch is not so much dissatisfied with his wandering as he is sensitive to opinion and a life he does not have. Coleeb proceeds to digress at great length, defending the life style of Duditch, gently scolding him for being too apologetic.

"Well, what if they do?" asked Coleeb. "Who are they to sit in judgment on how valuable or worthless your coming and goings are? They'd have a difficult case proving that they're better off than you. To have a family; not to have a family. To have a recognized career; not to have one. And so on. Well, what's the real difference? In one case, you do another set of things. In the other, you do another set of things. Either can be worthless. Either can be worthwhile. It all depends on what the given man makes of them. Or so it seems to me."

"That is very true," replied Costyve. "But" and then, having heard his own position so well defended, he began arguing the case of the settled people against himself, trying to show that they were more productive, more solid; they they had a function in life, that they fulfilled an obligation to society and constituted the backbone of the world; whereas he felt like a vagrant, useless appendage.[25]

This defense could well be autobiographical for Toomer. Certainly, it is prophetic. Toomer was gaining recognition and a certain amount of productivity was anticipated. From the information Toomer supplied in anthologies, periodicals, and literary notices since *Cane*, Toomer began a series of lengthy and ambitious works. From this period on, as the biographical section indicates, Toomer took a stance very similar to the comments of Coleeb. In his case, it did depend "on what the given man makes" of his choices in life.

The section concludes on a negative note since Coleeb, after recalling the eccentric behavior of Duditch, a person for whom he feels genuine affection, his mood changes from one of amusement to pathos. Duditch's antics actually constitute "the distorted wish for recognition." Hence, Coleeb undercuts his previous defense of Duditch. Duditch has the right to live his own life free from the censures of society but, nevertheless, the life Duditch has chosen for himself is fraught with inconsistencies and pettiness. The two friends agree to meet again at a tea to which both have been invited. It is to be given by one Constance Hanover at 4:30 that same afternoon.

When the two part, Coleeb begins a rather extended series of anecdotes about his friend, thus giving the narrator an opportunity to fill the reader in on various crucial facts concerning the life of Costyve Duditch. He likes to be recognized by bell-boys and passing acquaintances in his global journeys.

He had a way of going from city to city carefully selecting his hotels with the wish in mind: that after due period of absence, the doormen, the clerks, the porters, and the bell and elevator boys would remember him, salute him by name, complain that they had not seen him for ages and, in general, treat him as a visiting dignitary of great worth.[26]

He would go to elaborate ends to insure recognition, however. He never returned to a hotel a month after staying in it. On occasion he would wait for years only to be greeted as a treasured guest, which gave him the greatest pleasure. Duditch is most remembered, not for his personality, but for his tipping and extravagant tastes.

The narrative shifts from Coleeb to Duditch in the section which follows. It is developed in the manner of one day in the life of Duditch, reinforcing the observations made by Coleeb in the preceding section. Duditch carries out his plans for the day with clock-like precision. He arises after a typical sound sleep, showers, shaves, dresses. Two items are indispensable in his wardrobe—gray spats and a standing collar. These two items "served to give him an air of distinction wherever he went, and he was strongly inclined to wear them in warm weather and in hot climates."[27] Duditch prefers recognition and distinction over comfort and plain sensible dress. In another revealing statement, the narrator implies that Duditch may be a gelding, "never in his life to possess either mistress, lover, or wife."[28]

The next paragraph is an apologiac, containing positive references to the character of Duditch. His was an indefatigable spirit and his health was superior to most. He was a free spirit and "free to enjoy the unique strangeness and delights of each [place]" he visited.

After breakfast, Duditch made a practice of doing something to start the day in an orderly fashion. At 9:00 a.m., wherever he might be, Duditch would head for the business district. "He had a need to feel in touch with the forces and rhythms of men's tangible necessities." On this particular morning, Duditch visits his real estate agent and his stockbroker, with no change in either situation. Duditch is actually manufacturing tasks for himself and just as readily tires of them. Having time to kill before lunch, he wanders into Marshall Field where a finely wrought cut-glass bowl catches his eye. Unfortunately, he drops the bowl, smashing it to pieces, causing an immediate uproar. In consternation and embarrassment, Duditch hastens to pay for the bowl and exits the building.

Once outside, he feels the immediate need to flee Chicago itself. In an appropriate and moving analogy, Duditch thinks, "The city suddenly seemed to be in the same condition as the bowl. Always when he broke something, which he was constantly doing—either literally breaking something, or building up a scheme or a wish only to have it collapse on him—he felt...that he was the most clumsy person in the world."[29] The only thing to do before departing Chicago is to attend Miss Hanover's tea. Duditch flees to the shelter of his apartment to await the 4:30 rendezvous. It is here that the narrator exerts a distinctly humorous vein. Another of the stilted routines in Duditch's day is literary work after lunch. The narrator describes the notes, organized and collected over the years, which

Duditch hopes to shape into books. He already has selected the titles: one dealing with travel as a factor in the shaping of the cultured person, was to be called "The Influence of Travel on Personality." An alternate title for this book was: "How Travel Grooms the Person." A second volume concerning the love affairs of great men is to be entitled "When Love Was Great or Finesse in Love." The third volume on creativity has the working title "There is No Life Without Creation." All three are so mundane and insipid as to be intellectually devastating. In addition, Duditch, after washing away the grime of Chicago, begins to add to his collection of notes dressed in a gold-embroidered mandarin's cloak.

After the busy work of cataloging amidst interruptions for water, he begins the actual task of writing, the subject of which is the influence of travel on his personality. Duditch makes a point to include details of his earlier conversation with Coleeb. He manages to write a single page, a production which "moderately satisfied him and surprised him." This productivity, or lack of it, speaks for itself. Duditch is not a serious writer. Rather, he plays the role of author in much the same manner that he plays the role of entrepreneur and financier.

The final section closely details the events which take place at Miss Hanover's tea. The catalog of guests is both amusing and revealing. The guests include society women, a painter, a university professor, a critic of literature, a poet, an actress, a French diplomat and his wife, a college friend of Miss Hanover's, Coleeb, and Duditch. He is to be lionized on this occasion. Besieged by questions and curiosity, Duditch proceeds to describe the cities and adventures he has had all over the globe. The party is so attentive that he muses, "Indeed, they gave him such a sense of wholeness that both the cut-glass bowl and the entire city of Chicago were temporarily mended; he began to regret that he was leaving so soon. Here in this company, in his own town, the purpose and end of his wanderings seemed about to receive not only recognition but fulfillment."[30]

Duditch describes in some detail Toledo, Spain, and the El Greco he saw there, enthralling the attentive guests. Observing Duditch's role of lecturer, Coleeb makes some rather keen observations on the manner of his friend:

His tone contained an odd pleading apologetic persuasive quality mingled with a note which suggested that he was delighted with something, perhaps with life, and as pleased with himself as he dared be.[31]

With regard to the physical characteristics of Duditch, Coleeb observes:

His face alternated between three distinct expressions. One, a bright-eyed, eager, fertile expression. By this you could know, some seconds before its arrival, that an idea was coming to him. Then, once the idea had come and had been vocalized, sometimes with an odd confusion of words, sometimes with a surprising aptness and clarity, you could tell that it was going by the vacant look which swiftly descended on him. And, third, when quite gone, you could know this by the curious silent anticipatory way he would stare at you—an expression suggesting that though his own mind which only a minute before had been full was now blank, he expected either himself or you to say something of importance immediately.[32]

This observation is one of the most revealing in "Mr. Costyve Duditch." He is out of step with his audience, not really concerned with passing on relevant information. Rather, his mind is a kind of tabula rasa, his observations are as unconnected and thoroughly analyzed as the fruitless regimented life schedule he makes such an effort to fulfill.

The scene itself is shattered like the cut-glass bowl when the college friend asks Duditch what would happen to his body if he died in a far away land. He replies, "It would be disposed of according to the custom of the place."[33] Not content with this coldly objective statement, he states, "I have no doubt but what some fine morning a strange person using a foreign tongue will enter my room...and say, 'He's dead.'"[34] At the admonition, several listeners react, horrified at such coldness. They identify with the situation and shudder to think this might be their own fate. The party ends abruptly after the gloom of such reactions begins to pervade the heretofore festive atmosphere. Again, Duditch has broken something, this time the fragile decorum of tea-time etiquette. Unable to withstand the pervading atmosphere of pity, especially from Miss Hanover, Duditch beats a retreat in near panic. The cut-glass bowl incident is made even more analogous to the character of Duditch since "his world smashed to bits around him," he feels the necessity to flee Chicago. He rushes to his apartment, packs, and goes immediately to the railroad station. Costyve's departure is described as pathetic and "his spirit hugged itself in loneliness and he felt goaded by a thousand shattered hopes."[35] The narrative ends on an upbeat note. The narrator assures us that in the morning, Duditch will be his old self, renewed in spirit and humanitarianism. Duditch will, "bowl up the aisle, and out-beam all the men in the shaving room."[36]

"Mr. Costyve Duditch" is rather thin on plot, depending too much on the cut glass bowl imagery, but the narrative is well paced and tightly knit. Duditch is one of the more memorable characters in Toomer's canon. Toomer incorporates into this isolation themes of alienation and false, self-imposed sensibilities. The dual nature presented is also remarkably objective since Toomer himself must have identified totally with the dilemma of Duditch. He is an outsider, different, and an object of scorn. He is at the same time an admirable individualist. Caught between the two extremes, Duditch finally places too much emphasis on what society thinks of him, thus undercutting and "shattering" whatever admirable traits of intellect and individuality he might possess. In a perceptive comment, Michael Krasney offers some insight into Toomer's frame of reference and intent for "Mr. Costyve Duditch." He notes:

"Mr. Costyve Duditch" marks the beginning of his attempt to go beyond criticism and satire of America and even the representation of higher levels of consciousness implicit in "Winter on Earth," to an eventual consciousness.[37]

Toomer failed in his lofty ambition but "Mr. Costyve Duditch" was a step in the right direction. Its impact has not been muted by time nor the fact that it is one of his forgotten stories.

IV *"Blue Meridian"*

Toomer was successful in expressing his ideas in another genre, this time as a poet. He assumed that there was but one race and he devoted his final literary efforts to that end. His ideas on the formation of a new race in America have been incorporated into two poems, "Brown River, Smile" and "Blue Meridian." "Brown River, Smile" appeared in *Pagany* in 1932 and was later expanded into the longer poem and called "Blue Meridian," which was published in *The New Caravan*, edited by Alfred Kreymborg, Lewis Mumford, and Paul Rosenfield.

In "Blue Meridian," Toomer visualizes a "New America" which supersedes the old one that has been divided by the separation of men into races or national groups. Toomer says:

> It is a new America
> To be spiritualized by each new American,
> To be taken as a golden grain
> And lifted, as the wheat of our bodies,
> To matters uniquely man.[38]

He believes that Americans must outgrow the "unbecoming and enslaving behavior associated with our prejudices and preferences" which have impeded the progress of the nation. Americans and all countrymen must recognize that they obey the same laws and have the same goals and objectives and that all mankind possesses an "essence identical in all." Toomer visualizes America as a land in which "wave after wave" of European races have joined to grow towns on the rich soil of America; these towns, however, after a "swift achievement," have given way to a world of "crying men and hard women, a city of goddam and Jehovah,/ Baptized in finance."[39]

Echoing ideas of D. H. Lawrence, Toomer deplores the statement that bloods of men in America cannot be mixed and that men have not been able to experience "birth above the body." Lawrence had maintained that modern man and woman no longer experienced true communion with one another because of the "death drive" of civilization and that death of the old ego-self and a resurrection of the bodily self were needed. Toomer pursues a similar theme in "Blue Meridian," that modern civilization has been responsible for the chaotic condition of the present-day world. He believes that a new people for whom America is waiting will throw off the separateness that has developed because of the different waves of races that have come to America:

> When the Spirit of mankind conceived
> A New World in America, and dreamed
> The human structure rising from this base,
> The land was as a vacant house to new inhabitants,
> A vacuum compelled by Nature to be filled.
> Spirit could not wait to time-select,
> Weighing in wisdom each piece,
> Fitting each right thing into each right place,
> But had to act, trusting the vision of the possible,
> Had to bring vast life to this vast plot,
>
> Drawing, in waves of inhabitation,
> All the people of the earth,
> Later to weed out, organize, assimilate.
> And thus we are—

> Gathered by the snatch of accident,
> Selected with the speed of fate,
> The alien and the belonging,
> All belonging now,
> Not yet made one and aged.[40]

"I would give my life," continues the poet of Toomer's poem, to see the words "understanding, conscience, and ability" inscribed upon the life of everyone's consciousness so that all who wish might be able to "unbend dreams." He reminds the reader that lives of Americans are blighted by "mistakes and hates" that rush out of the past blinding and sweeping.

The "pioneers and puritans," the poet says, who have passed on to us our legacy where themselves indentured; they have condemned those whom they subjugated to "Fill space and pass time/Within a prison system." And he adds:

> Nor can we eat, though food is here,
> Nor can we breathe, though the universe is air,
> Nor can we move, though the planet speeds,
> Nor can we circulate, though Nature flows,
> Nor can we love and bear love's fruit
> Though we are living and life is everywhere.[41]

"Americans," he continues, "must outgrow themselves and their old place" and fix the "symbol of universal man" as their center of gravity. The poet's final plea is to "uncase the races" from the unbecoming and enslaving behavior" and to eliminate "prejudices and preferences," for, he says, all mankind is of the human race:

> Uncase, unpod whatever impedes, until,
> Having realized pure consciousness of being
> Sensing, feeling and understanding
> That we are beings,
> Co-existing with others in an inhabited universe,
> We will be free to use rightly with reason
> Our own and other human functions.[42]

The final section of the poem contains a narrative in which the poet relates how he, who had been praised and honored by the public, was attacked by public scavengers who had found a "river flowing backward into its source," obviously a reference to the ancestry of the poet. He tells us:

> I held a fair position as men rate things,
> Even enviable—
> I could taste flavors in a grain of sand,
> My eyes saw loveliness,
> And I learned to peal the wind,
> In short, I was a lucky fellow,
> People shook my hand, said nice things,
> And sometimes slapped me on the back;
> Curious, then, that I, of all people
> In the month of the nasty mouth,
> Should have found myself caught
> In a backbay leased by public and private scavengers;
> Such was the case—but I found
> A river flowing backward to its source.[43]

The poet concludes that the "new people" of America will mix their bloods, that they will suffer and create and "live in body," and that no man will be branded as a slave or a peon. The African races and the great red race will join with the waves of races from Europe and "aid the operation of the cosmos":

> We who exist today are the new people,
> Born of elevated rock and lifted branches,
> A race called the Americans—
> Not to call this name but to live the reality,
> Not to stop at it, but to respond to man;
> And we are the old people; we are witnesses
> That behind us there extends
> An unbroken chain of ancestors, linking us
> To all who ever lived and will live;
> Of millions of fathers through a million years
> We are the breathing receptacles.[44]

The poet has faith that modern man will triumph over the "prejudices and preferences" which have been practiced in the past. The black and the white, the people of the East and West, will all join to give rise to the "blue man," who represents those who have struggled through the ages to give rise to a new people.

This dream of a world in which all racial barriers would be eliminated represents the culmination of Toomer's views on race. Harassed by "public scavengers," as he called those who trace an individual's ancestry back to its sources, Toomer adopted the view that a new race had developed in America. This race, he said, could best exist in a new world which disregards racial ties.

"Blue Meridian" incorporates Toomer's final statement of his theory of the racial composition of America. It contains his plea that he be accepted as an Amerian author and that his work be judged on its own intrinsic merits. This poem, which appeared in 1936, seems to be his last published creative work of consequence. In his earliest writing, he had attempted to treat black life as it existed in America as an integral part of the historical pattern of America. Then, he had found his identity with the black race and had satisfied his own emotional needs through writing about blacks. But in time, he expressed the belief that a literary artist should not limit his work's subject matter to any one group, in his case, the black race. He did not want his work to be labelled as "Negro literature." He insisted that literature ought to be on the plane of art and intelligence and that an author's racial identity ought not be considered when his work was evaluated.

It was useless for Toomer to try to disassociate his name from the black race. His singular success with *Cane* and his inclusion in discussions of works by black American authors could never be forgotten. His attempts to deny the existence of the black race in America as an entity led him into obscurity. Toomer lost contact with the world of reality. Rather than confine his literary endeavors to the literature of the black group, Toomer developed a new style, a half-convincing style that bordered on the psychological and mystical. His later work was unconvincing. The promise that was shown by *Cane* was never fulfilled.

CHAPTER 5

Some Conclusions

THE testimonials on the dust jacket of the 1967 University Place reprint of the original *Cane* bear witness to Jean Toomer's present stature in American literature. Robert Bone called *Cane* "the most impressive product of the Negro Renaissance, it ranks with Richard Wright's *Native Son* and Ralph Ellison's *Invisible Man* as a measure of the Negro novelist's highest achievement." Langston Hughes describing its success says "...(excepting the work of DuBois) *Cane* contains the finest prose written by a Negro in America. And, like the singing of Robeson, it is truly racial." Arna Bontemps notes that "...certainly no other volume of poetry or fiction or both had come close to expressing the ethos of the Negro in the Southern setting as *Cane* did." Each remembered *Cane* as a harbinger of a new, more productive era in the history of Afro-American literature. Moreover, Bone, Hughes, and Bontemps were continually impressed with the talent Jean Toomer displayed with his first book, an almost unprecedented acknowledgment.[1]

Since *Cane* was obviously not a financial success, with less than a thousand copies sold, it must have left a special mark on these critics and authors. With the availability of the recent paperback editions, *Cane* now reaches a much larger audience, is proving a financially successful venture, and once again is beginning to exert a wide influence on readers just now becoming acquainted with the work.[2] Toomer would have appreciated the attention given to him, but one doubts that he would have altered the course of his career. Toomer was not in pursuit of success. Rather he sought the truth—truth about himself, his contemporaries, and the society in which he chose to live. Toomer failed, as all great artists do, but when one reads through the mountains of material he left behind, one cannot help but be struck by the effort which must have gone into his compositions after *Cane*. Many of his selections are virtually impenetrable. Toomer wrote and apparently extensively revised hundreds of poems after 1923. Some are very short; others, like "Bride of Air," are of some length. The common thread in the poems is a distinct opaqueness. The reader is puzzled by Toomer's intent. The unpublished novels, "Eight Day World" as representative, were often revised but still lack a solidarity of purpose and become muddled in philosophical sidestepping. The autobiographies, "Earth Being" as an example, are likewise difficult to follow because the thread of thought is so often tangential to the material presently under discussion. This is not to say nothing of importance survives. This is simply not the case. But, one must bear in mind the failure and small successes Toomer engendered after *Cane.* It would seem that later on words, the very language itself, failed Jean Toomer. He did not fail with words. Some selections and portions of unfinished material are thought-provoking and oftentimes exciting as one recognizes the great mind at work here, molding an idea into a translatable form.

One may also take another approach to the evaluation of Jean Toomer's career. It is justifiable to say that if he wrote *Cane* he was capable and talented enough to have left a large body of published work. Why did he not even approach the brilliance of *Cane* in his later writing? Did he go off the deep end, spending too much time gathering information of a psychological and philosophic nature? He did write about these subjects which so deeply interested him, but he was never able to find a proper vehicle for his findings. Arna Bontemps notes that Charles S. Johnson, an entrepreneur of the Harlem Renaissance, spoke at Howard University. The subject was a review of the Harlem Renaissance after twenty-five years. Johnson acknowledged that Jean Toomer was a harbinger with *Cane,* but "Toomer flashed like a meteor across the sky, then sank from view. The common judgment became an acknowledgment that Jean Toomer probably wasted his talent, squandering his creative efforts on tangential material not related to his own roots. When Toomer denied his heritage, preferring to be known as an American rather than a black writer, did he lose his creative strength? No one will ever know with any degree of certainty. Another factor may have been his disappointment with sales and its reception by blacks. Langston Hughes described the situation aptly when he said, "The colored people did not praise it. The white people did not buy it."[3]

The truth probably lies somewhere in between. Toomer did publish "Easter," "Mr. Costyve Duditch," and the long poem "Blue

Meridian," among the others noted. Each has merit and bears closer scrutiny. Toomer worked hard at his profession, very hard, but he had lost touch. The touch he lost may have been racial, artistic, or psychological or a combination of the three. His was a talent diverted from the mainstream. This approach was consistent with the composition of *Cane*. After all, the publication of his masterpiece was certainly to catch the mainstream, readers and critics alike, by surprise. There has been nothing like *Cane* before or since. Our judgment of Jean Toomer must rest with this admission.

Toomer criticism is rapidly expanding, judging from the number of articles and dissertations directly and indirectly related to Jean Toomer and the Harlem Renaissance appearing in PMLA bibliographies. Toomer criticism has also matured quite rapidly. The early studies dealt largely in generalities about *Cane* or were severely limited to analysis of individual pieces excerpted from the body of *Cane*. It should also be noted that such popular selections as "Blood Burning Moon" and "Karintha" are frequently included in anthologies of American and Afro-American literature. This method of popularizing Toomer's material has one serious drawback. It tends to fragment and oftentimes blur the cohesive elements in *Cane* itself.

The one book-length study of *Cane* presently available is Frank Durham's *The Merrill Studies in Cane*. There are some excellent studies in books. Darwin Turner's *In a Minor Chord* is one such text, as is Robert Bone's *The Negro Novel in America*, although it is more generalized. Three unpublished dissertations contribute much to Toomer scholarship. Mabel Dillard's "Jean Toomer: Herald of the Negro Renaissance" (1967) was the first major study of Toomer and offers valuable insights. Arlene Crewdson's "Invisibility: A Study of the Works of Toomer, Wright, and Ellison" (1974) contains an excellent working bibliography. Michael Krasney's "Jean Toomer and the Quest for Consciousness" (1972) explores Toomer's philosophical and psychological interests at great and insightful length.

Three Toomer studies are outstanding: John M. Reilly's "The Search for Black Redemption: Jean Toomer's *Cane*"; Darwin Turner's "Introduction" to *Cane*, and Catherine Innes's "The University of Jean Toomer's *Cane*" offer exciting and provocative concepts.

With regard to future Toomer studies, several important projects ought to be undertaken. With the wealth of material housed at Fisk

University available to the serious student, a thorough biography of Toomer can and should be undertaken. This biography would clear up many questions concerning Toomer's later years. Extant Toomer poetry needs cataloging and the best selections deserve publication in book-length form. Finally, the letters of Jean Toomer are of great value to students of the period and rightfully deserve publication in book form. These three areas of study are the most crucial and deserve immediate attention.

Notes and References

Chapter One

1. Jean Toomer, "Outline of Autobiography" (Unpublished manuscript, ca. 1934) Toomer Collection, Fisk University Library, p. 15.
2. Ibid., pp. 50-51.
3. Ibid.
4. Ibid., pp. 55-56.
5. Ibid.
6. Letter from Lola Ridge to Jean Toomer, dated December 12, 1922, Toomer Collection, Fisk University Library.
7. Charles Waddell Chestnut, "Post-Bellum—Pre-Harlem," *Crisis* 28 (June 1931): 194.
8. John McClure to Jean Toomer, letter dated June 30, 1922, Toomer Collection, Fisk University Library.
9. Toomer, "Outline of Autobiography," pp. 55-56.
10. Sherwood Anderson to Jean Toomer, letter dated September 1922, Toomer Collection, Fisk University Library.
11. Jean Toomer to Sherwood Anderson, letter dated December 28, 1922, Toomer Collection, Fisk University Library.
12. Extract from a letter from Jean Toomer to Sherwood Anderson, dated December 29, 1922, Toomer Collection, Fisk University Library.
13. Jean Toomer to Sherwood Anderson (no date) Toomer Collection, Fisk University Library.
14. Extract from an undated letter from Jean Toomer to Waldo Frank (ca. 1922) Toomer Collection, Fisk University Library.
15. Extract from a letter from Jean Toomer to Waldo Frank, dated August 15, 1921, Waldo Frank Collection, University of Pennsylvania Library.
16. Extract from a letter from Jean Toomer to Waldo Frank, dated August 1922, Toomer Collection, Fisk University Library.
17. Extract from a letter from Jean Toomer to Waldo Frank, dated August 24, 1922, Toomer Collection, Fisk University Library.
18. Extract from a letter from Jean Toomer to Lola Ridge, dated August 20, 1922, Toomer Collection, Fisk University Library.
19. Toomer, "Outline of Autobiography," p. 57.
20. Ibid.

21. Extract from an undated letter from Jean Toomer to Waldo Frank, Toomer Collection, Fisk University Library.

22. Ibid.

23. Waldo Frank, Foreword to *Cane* (New York: Boni and Liveright, 1923), p. ix.

24. Alfred Kreymborg, *Our Singing Strength: An Outline of Amrican Poetry*, 1620-1930 (New York: Macaulay, 1929), p. 575.

25. Edward J. O'Brien, "The Best Short Stories of 1923," *Boston Evening Transcript*, December 1, 1923, Part VI, p. 1.

26. Sherwood Anderson to Jean Toomer, letter dated December 12, 1922, Jean Toomer Collection, Fisk University Library.

27. Extract from a letter from Gorham Munson to Waldo Frank, dated October 19, 1922, Waldo Frank papers, Van Pelt Library, University of Pennsylvania.

28. Gorham B. Munson, "The Significance of Jean Toomer," *Opportunity* 3 (September 1925): 261.

29. Robert Littell, "Cane," *New Republic* 137 (December 26, 1923): 126.

30. Ibid.

31. Paul Rosenfeld, "Jean Toomer," *Men Seen* (New York: Dial, 1925), pp. 228-29.

32. Ibid, pp. 232-33.

33. Extract from a letter from Claude Barnett to Jean Toomer, dated April 23, 1923, Toomer Collection, Fisk University Library.

34. Extract from a letter from Jean Toomer to Claude Barnett, dated April 29, 1923, Toomer Collection, Fisk University Library.

35. W. E. B. DuBois, "The Younger Literary Movement," *Crisis* 27 (February 1924): 162.

36. William Stanley Braithwaite, "The Negro in Literature," *Crisis* 28 (September 1924): 207.

37. J. Saunders Redding, "American Negro Literature," *American Scholar* 128 (June 12, 1949): 711.

38. George W. Jacobs, "Negro Authors Must Eat," *Nation* 128 (June 12, 1949): 711.

39. Extract of a letter from Jean Toomer to Claude McKay, dated August 19, 1922, Toomer Collection, Fisk University Library.

40. Extract from a letter from Alain Locke to Jean Toomer, dated September 18, 1923, Toomer Collection, Fisk University Library.

41. Gorham Munson, "The Significance of Jean Toomer," p. 262.

42. Ibid., pp. 262-63.

43. Yvonne DuPee to Jean Toomer, Letter dated April 4, 1932, Toomer Collection, Fisk University Library.

44. Jean Toomer. "A Fact and Some Fictions," Toomer Collection, Fisk University Library.

45. Marjorie Content Toomer to Mabel Dillard, letter dated March 11, 1967.

46. Interview of Mabel Dillard with Mrs. Marion Fuson at Fisk University, Nashville, Tennessee, February 1967.

Chapter Two

1. Addison Gayle, *The Way of the New World: The Black Novel in America*, (New York: 1975), p. 98.

2. Abraham Chapman, ed., *Black Voice* (New York: 1968), p. 83.

3. Bernard Bell, "A Key to the Poems in *Cane*," *CLA Journal* 14 (March 1971): 252.

4. Edward W. Waldron, "The Search for Identity in Jean Toomer's 'Esther,'" *CLA Journal* 14 (March 1971): 227.

5. Darwin Turner, "Introduction," *Cane* (New York: Liveright, 1975), p. xxi.

6. Jean Toomer, *Cane* (New York: Boni and Liveright, 1923; New York: University Place Press, 1967), p. 21.

7. Houston Baker, *Singers At Daybreak: Studies in Black American Literature* (Washington, D.C.: Howard University Press, 1974), p. 8.

8. Robert Bone, *The Negro Novel in America* (Revised edition; New Haven: Yale University Press, 1965), p. 82.

9. Toomer, *Cane*, p. 5.

10. Baker, p. 58.

11. *Cane*, p. 13. The paperback edition (New York: Liveright, 1975) substitutes "cane" for "corn." This is probably correct.

12. Ibid., p. 14.

13. Ibid., p. 18.

14. Ibid., p. 17.

15. Ibid., pp. 24-25.

16. Ibid., p. 32.

17. Ibid., p. 29.

18. The word "dictie" is defined as stylish, high class, bossy, and snobbish. *The Dictionary of American Slang*, compiled by Harold Wentworth and Stuart Flexner (New York: Crowell, 1967), p. 146. It has a variant spelling of "dicty," origin unknown, meaning uppish and conceited. *A Supplement to the Oxford English Dictionary*, ed. R. W. Burchfield. Vol. I [A-G] (Oxford: Clarendon Press, 1972), p. 795.

19. *Cane*, p. 38.

20. Bone, p. 84.

21. Toomer, *Cane*, p. 40.

22. Ibid., p. 37.

23. Ibid., p. 39.

24. Ibid., pp. 42-43.

25. Ibid., p. 47.

26. Ibid., pp. 43-44.

27. Ibid., p. 45.

28. Ibid., p. 37.
29. Ibid., p. 39.
30. Ibid., p. 51.
31. Ibid.
32. Ibid.
33. Ibid., p. 52.
34. Ibid., pp. 59-60.
35. Crewdson, p. 50.
36. Toomer, *Cane*, p. 4.
37. Quoted in Alain Locke's *The New Negro* (New York: Boni and Liveright, 1925), p. 51.
38. Toomer, *Cane*, pp. 10-11.
39. Ibid., p. 36.
40. Ibid., pp. 16-20.
41. Ibid., pp. 51-67.
42. Bone, p. 87.
43. Toomer, *Cane*, p. 71.
44. A number of critics have noted this similarity.
45. *Cane*, p. 78.
46. Ibid., p. 80.
47. Ibid., pp. 80-81.
48. Ibid., p. 81.
49. Ibid., p. 83.
50. Ibid., p. 86.
51. Ibid., p. 88.
52. Crewdson, p. 61.
53. *Cane*, p. 98.
54. Ibid., pp. 105-106.
55. Ibid., p.108.
56. Ibid., p. 113.
57. Ibid., p. 117.
58. Extract from a letter from Jean Toomer to Lola Ridge. August 10, 1922, Toomer Collection, Fisk University Library.
59. *Cane*, p. 119.
60. Ibid., p. 21.
61. Ibid., p. 103.
62. Ibid., p. 73.
63. Ibid.
64. Ibid., p. 74.
65. Ibid., p. 75.
66. Darwin Turner. "Jean Toomer's *Cane*," *Negro Digest* 18:3 (January 1969): 61.
67. Arlene Crewdson. *Invisibility: A Study of the Works of Toomer, Wright, and Ellison* (Unpublished Dissertation: Loyola University of Chicago, 1974), p. 59.

68. *Cane*, p. 74.

69. Extract of a letter from Jean Toomer to Waldo Frank, dated December 12, 1922. Toomer Collection, Fisk University Library.

70. *Cane*, pp. 137-38.

71. Crewdson, p. 85.

72. *Cane*, pp. 152-53.

73. Ibid., p. 157.

74. Ibid., pp. 185-86.

75. Ibid., pp. 200-201.

76. Ibid., p. 188.

77. Ibid.

78. Ibid., pp. 171-172.

79. Ibid., p. 223.

80. Ibid., p. 219.

81. Ibid., pp. 231-32.

82. Ibid., p. 205.

83. Ibid., p. 158.

84. Bone, p. 88.

85. *Cane*, p. 2.

86. Ibid., p. 1.

87. Ibid., p. 13.

88. Ibid., p. 18.

89. Ibid., pp. 161-62.

90. Toomer, "Outline of Autobiography," pp. 58-59. Jean Toomer Collection: Fisk University Library.

91. David Littlejohn, *Black on White: A Critical Survey of Writing by American Negroes* (New York: Grossman, 1966), p. 170.

Chapter Three

1. Alfred Kreymborg, *Our Singing Strength* (New York: Macauley, 1929), p. 575.

2. Extract from an undated letter from Jean Toomer to Waldo Frank (ca. 1922), Toomer Collection, Fisk University Library.

3. Extract from an undated letter from Jean Toomer to Waldo Frank (ca. 1922), Toomer Papers, Fisk University Library.

4. Extract from an undated letter from Waldo Frank to Jean Toomer (ca. 1922), Toomer Papers, Fisk University Library.

5. David Littlejohn, *Black on White: A Critical Survey of Writing by American Negroes* (New York: Grossman, 1966), p. 58.

6. "Just American," *Time* 19:1 (March 28, 1932): 19.

7. Ibid.

8. Extract from a letter from Jean Toomer to Miss Nancy Cunard, dated February 8, 1932, Toomer Collection, Fisk University Library.

9. Extracts from a letter from Jean Toomer to James Weldon Johnson, dated July 11, 1930, and from an undated letter to Miss Catherine Latimer (ca. 1934) of the New York Public Library, Toomer Papers, Fisk University Library.

10. S. P. Fullinwider, "Jean Toomer: Lost Generation, or Negro Renaissance?" *Phylon* 28 (Summer 1967): 396.

11. Jean Toomer, "The Negro Emergent" (Unpublished essay, ca. 1925), Toomer Collection, Fisk University Library.

12. Ibid., pp. 7-8.

13. Ibid., p. 10.

14. Jean Toomer, "Race Problems and Modern Society," in *Problems of Civilization* (Vol. VII of *Man and His World* series), ed. Baker Brownell (New York: 1929), p. 78.

15. Ibid., p. 108.

16. Toomer, *Essentials* (Chicago: Lakeside Press, 1931), p. XIV.

17. Extract from a letter from Jean Toomer to Miss Catherine Latimer (ca. 1934), Toomer Collection, Fisk University Library.

Chapter Four

1. Michael Krasney. "Jean Toomer and the Quest for Consciousness" (Unpublished Dissertation, Univ. of Wisconsin, 1972), pp. 110-11.

2. "Easter," *Little Review*, Spring 1925, pp. 3-7.

3. Ibid., p. 4.

4. Ibid.

5. Ibid.

6. Ibid.

7. Ibid., p. 5.

8. Ibid., p. 6.

9. Ibid., p. 7.

10. "Notes on Contributors," *The Second American Caravan*, ed. Alfred Kreymborg et al. (New York: Macauley Company, 1928).

11. Ibid., p. 695.

12. Ibid., p. 696.

13. Ibid., p. 698.

14. Ibid., p. 700.

15. Ibid., p. 703.

16. Ibid., p. 713.

17. Ibid.

18. Ibid., p. 714.

19. Ibid., p. 715.

20. Krasney, p. 134.

21. "Mr. Costyve Duditch," *Dial* 85:6 (December 1925): 460-76.

22. Ibid., p. 460.
23. Ibid.
24. Ibid., p. 463.
25. Ibid., pp. 463-64.
26. Ibid., p. 465.
27. Ibid., p. 466.
28. Ibid.
29. Ibid., p. 468.
30. Ibid., p. 472.
31. Ibid., p. 473.
32. Ibid., pp. 473-74.
33. Ibid., p. 474.
34. Ibid., p. 475.
35. Ibid., p. 476.
36. Ibid.
37. Krasney, p. 154.
38. Jean Toomer, "The Blue Meridian," *The New Caravan*, ed. Alfred Kreymborg et al. (New York: Macauley Company, 1936), p. 638.
39. Ibid.
40. Ibid., p. 637.
41. Ibid., p. 640.
42. Ibid., p. 645.
43. Ibid., pp. 646-47.
44. Ibid., pp. 651-52.

Chapter Five

1. Jean Toomer, *Cane* (New York: University Place Press, 1967). All references are from this source.
2. The only edition presently in print is *Cane* (New York: Liveright, 1975), but it is readily available and in some demand.
3. Jean Toomer, *Cane* (New York: University Place Press, 1967). Dustjacket quote.

Selected Bibliography

PRIMARY SOURCES

1. Books

Cane. New York: Boni and Liveright, 1923.
Essentials. Chicago: Lakeside Press, 1931.

2. Short Stories

"Becky." *Liberator* 5:10 (October 1922). Included in *Cane.*
"Carma." *Liberator* 5:19 (September 1922). Included in *Cane.*
"Fern." *Little Review* 9:3 (Autumn 1922). Included in *Cane.*
"Kabnis." *Broom* (August 1923). Included in *Cane.*
"Karintha." *Broom* (January 1923). Included in *Cane.*
"Easter." *Little Review* (Spring 1925).
"Mr. Costyve Duditch." *Dial* 85:6 (December 1928).
"Winter on Earth." *The Second American Caravan* Ed. Alfred Kreymborg et al. New York: Macauley Company, 1928.
"York Beach." *The New American Caravan.* Ed. Alfred Kreymborg et al. New York: Macauley Company, 1929.
"York Beach." *The New American Caravan.* Ed. Alfred Kreymborg et al. New York: Macauley Company, 1929.

3. Poems

"As the Eagle Soars." *Crisis* (April 1932).
"Blue Meridian." *The New American Caravan.* Ed. Alfred Kreymborg et al. New York: W. W. Norton, 1936.
"Brown River Smile." *Pagany* III (January-March 1932).
"Georgia Dusk." *Liberator* 5 (September 1922). Included in *Cane.*
"Gum." *Chapbook* (April 1923).
"Harvest Song." *Double Dealer* 4 (December 1922). Included in *Cane.*
"Her Lips Are Cooper Wine." *S4N* 26 (May 1923). Included in *Cane.*
"Nora." *Double Dealer* 4 (September 1922). Included in *Cane.* Entitled "Calling Jesus."
"November Cotton Flower." *Nomad* (Summer 1923). Included in *Cane.*

"Seventh Street." *Broom* (December 1922). Included in *Cane.*
"Song of the Sun." *Crisis* (April 1922). Included in *Cane.*
"Storm Ending." *Double Dealer* 4 (September 1922). Included in *Cane.*
"White Arrow." *Dial* (July 1929).

4. Miscellaneous

"Reflections." *Dial* (April 1929). Aphorisms.
Balo. Plays of Negro Life. Ed. Alain Locke and Montgomery Gregory.
    New York: Harper's, 1927.
"Oxen Cart and Warfare." *Little Review* (Autumn, Winter 1924-25).
    Criticism.
"Race Problems and Modern Society." *Man and His World.* Ed. Baker
    Brownell. New York: D. Van Nostrand, 1929.
The Flavor of Man. William Penn Lecture, 1949. Pamphlet.

5. Unpublished Novels, Toomer Collection, Fisk University

"Caromb" (1932).
"The Gallonwerps" (1927; revised 1933).
"Transatlantic" (1929; revised as "Eight Day World," 1933; revised 1934).

6. Unpublished Poetry

"Blue Meridian and Other Poems" (1933).
"Bride of Air" (1931).

7. Unpublished Stories

"Drachman" (1928).
"Love on a Train" (1928).
"Lump" (1928).
"Mr. Limph Krok's Famous L'Pride" (1930).
"Two Professors" (1930).
"Withered Skin of Berries" (1930).

8. Unpublished Autobiographies

"Autobiography" (1936).
"Earth Being" (1930).
"Incredible Journey" (1945).
"Outline of an Autobiography" (1946).

SECONDARY SOURCES

ACKLEY, DONALD G. "Themes and Vision in Jean Toomer's *Cane*." *Studies in Black Literature* 1 (1970): 56-58. A general analysis of the major themes in *Cane*. Ackley suggests that *Cane* is more organized than previously believed.

BELL, BERNARD. "A Key to the Poems in *Cane*," *CLA Journal* 14 (March 1971): 251-58. Explicates in detail the poems in Parts One and Two and discusses their functins with the novel as a whole. Bell argues that these poems "communicate the spiritual core of *Cane* and suggest the metaphysical forces necesary to bring the crass materialism of American society and the sensuality of man's nature into harmony."

———. "Portrait of the Artist as High Priest of Soul: Jean Toomer's *Cane*." *Black World* (September 1974): 4-19, 92-97. A detailed, thorough, and perceptive analysis that covers many aspects of form and meaning in *Cane*. Bell interprets this "poetic novel" in terms of Toomer's "mystical theory of life" and his desire to attain "a higher level of consciousness of self," arguing that the work depicts "a deeply religious quest: a search for the truth about Man, God, and America that takes its nameless poet/narrator on a circular journey of self-discovery."

BONE, ROBERT. *The Negro Novel in America*. Rev. ed. New Haven, Connecticut: Yale Univer. Press, 1965. Contains a valuable discussion of the major themes, the literary techniques, the overall design of *Cane*. Bone emphasizes Toomer's humanistic and primitivistic protest against modern industrial society, his experimentation with style and symbolism, and his historical importance as a literary innovator. According to Bone, Toomer was the "only Negro writer of the 1920's who participated on equal terms in the creation of the modern idiom" in literature.

BONTEMPS, ARNA. "The Harlem Renaissance." *Saturday Review of Literature* 30 (March 22, 1947): 12-13, 44. A general overview of the impact of the Harlem Renaissance. Toomer is mentioned briefly.

———. "The Negro Renaissance: Jean Toomer and the Harlem Writers of the 1920's." In *Anger, and Beyond: The Negro Writer in the United States*. Ed. Herbert Hill. New York: Harper and Row, 1966, pp. 20-36. An important and wide-ranging discussion of Toomer's career that explores the "literary mystery" of Toomer's failure as a writer after the publication of *Cane*. In arguing that Toomer "turned his back on greatness" when he denied his race, Bontemps suggests that Toomer should be seen as a "representative" figure whose "dilemmas and frustrations as a writer are equally the dilemmas and frustrations of the Negro writers who have since emerged."

BRICKNELL, HERSELL. "On *Cane*." *Literary Review* (December 8, 1923): 333. An influential review praising *Cane* as a work of artistic merit.

CANCEL, RAFAEL A. "Male and Female Interrelationship in Toomer's *Cane*." *Negro American Literature Forum* 5 (Spring 1971): 25-31. Traces a "cycle" in Cane which culminates in a reconciliation of "male and female through an acceptance of the past and the healing contact of the soil." Offers fine interpretations of individual narratives and some useful generalizations concerning parallels between Toomer and the Agrarians.

CHAPMAN, ABRAHAM. "The Harlem Renaissance in Literary History." *CLA Journal* 11 (September 1967): 38-58. Deplores the inadequate treatment of the Negro Renaissance in standard literary histories and specialized studies of the 1920s, asserting that this renaissance was "a landmark in Negro self-expression in America." Quotes Richard Wright on Toomer's importance for later Negro writers.

CHASE, PATRICIA. "The Women in *Cane*." *CLA Journal* 14 (March 1971): 259-73. Emphasizes the archetypal qualities of Toomer's female characters, arguing that Toomer's "vision of womankind" culminates in Carrie K.

CREWDSON, ARLENE J. "Invisibility: A Study of the Works of Toomer, Wright and Ellison." Diss. Loyola Univ. of Chicago, 1974. Crewdson analyzes, evaluates, and summarizes critical theories attributed to the authors, and attempts to place Toomer, Wright, and Ellison in the realm of American letters. This study has the added advantage of a fairly comprehensive bibliography, Toomer in particular.

"Cultural Outpouring of the Harlem Renaissance," *Life* 65 (December 5, 1968): 100-101. Mentions Toomer as one of several Renaissance writers whose works "articulated the anguish of the New Negro" and "entered the mainstream of a particularly productive period of American letters."

DILLARD, MABEL M. "Jean Toomer: Herald of the Negro Renaissance." Diss. Ohio Univer. 1967. The first major study of Jean Toomer. Dillard asserts that Cane was a pivotal work in the launching of the Harlem Renaissance. Toomer was one of the most gifted and experimental writers of the period. She makes a case for *Cane* as a classic of American Literature.

DUNCAN, BOWIE. "Jean Toomer's *Cane*: A Modern Black Oracle." *CLA Journal* 15 (March 1972): 323-33. Argues that a modern concept of reality is relative, multi-faceted, and fundamentally ambiguous lies behind Toomer's departure from "linear" composition and his presentation of "unending variations on certain themes."

DURHAM, FRANK, comp. *The Merrill Studies in Cane.* Columbus, Ohio: Charles E. Merrill Publishing Co., 1971. An excellent compilation that admirably fulfills the stated purpose of bringing together "the documents which will enable the reader to trace the history of *Cane*'s literary reputation." Includes reviews, critical essays, excerpts from longer works, introductions to editions, and other materials essential for the scholarly and critical study of *Cane*.

──────. "The Poetry Society of South Carolina's Turbulent Year: Self-Interest, Atheism, and Jean Toomer." *Southern Humanities Review* 5 (1971): 76-80. An anecdotal commentary concerning Jean Toomer's disquieting relationship with the Poetry Society of South Carolina.

FARRISON, W. EDWARD. "Jean Toomer's *Cane* Again." *CLA Journal* 15 (March 1972): 295-302. Discusses the novel's reputation and influence, claiming that "the influences by which *Cane* has been said to have been affected and the influence attributed to it have been generally... overemphasized." Also comments on aspects of form, structure, and style.

FAULKNER, HOWARD. "The Buried Life: Jean Toomer's *Cane*." *Studies in Black Literature* 7 (Winter 1976): 1-5. Develops the point that Toomer's characters have a "buried life" which demands "release" and creative "expression" but which is often frustrated by inner "fragmentation." Also comments on the novel's "symbolic imagery."

FRANK, WALDO. Foreword. *Cane*, by Jean Toomer. New York: University Place Press, 1967, pp. vii-xi. *Cane* is a masterpiece of lyric beauty. "It is a harbinger of the South's literary maturity: of its emergence from the obsession put upon its mind by the unending racial crisis—an obsession from which writers have made their indirect escape through sentimentalism, exoticism, polemic, 'problem' fiction, and moral melodrama."

FULLINWIDER, S. P. "Jean Toomer: Lost Generation, or Negro Renaissance?" *Phylon* 27 (Fourth Quarter 1966): 396-403. An important and stimulating discussion of Toomer's intellectual and artistic development that emphasizes Toomer's modern sense of alienation and his his modern quest for "an identity-giving absolute." Fullinwider argues that "after writing *Cane*, Toomer fled from reality, found his absolute and clung to it," with the result that he ceased to be a fine creative artist capable of expressing "modern man's restlessness and lostness."

GLOSTER, HUGH M. *Negro Voices in American Fiction.* Chapel Hill, North Carolina: Univ. of North Carolina, 1948. Gives a general overview of *Cane*'s themes, emphasizing the novel's originality. Finds *Cane* "noteworthy because of its departure from argumentation and apologetics in the treatment of interracial subject matter as well as because of its prefiguration of Southern realism and Negro self-revelation."

GOEDE, WILLIAM J. "Jean Toomer's Ralph Kabnis: Portrait of the Negro Artist as a Young man." *Phylon* 30 (First Quarter 1969): 73-85. Offers fine interpretations of "Box Seat," "Kabnis," and other stories in *Cane*, with some shrewd comments on Toomer's symbolism.

According to Goede, Ralph Kabnis is "Toomer's portrait of the Negro writer who, like the Invisible Man, is trying somehow to reduce his chaotic impressions and fears of Negro life into metaphor."

GRANT, SISTER MARY KATHRYN. "Images of Celebration in *Cane*." *Negro American Literature Forum* 5 (Spring 1971): 32-34, 36. Asserts that although *Cane* is a novel of "searching and sadness, pain and death...there is an underlying spirit of hopeful celebration." Finds that "images of celebration" are usually associated with the South, and that they occur more frequently in the novel's first and third sections than in the second.

HOLMES, EUGENE. "Jean Toomer—Apostle of Beauty." *Opportunity* 10 (August 1932): 252-54, 260. An interesting early assessment attributing Toomer's historical importane as a Negro poet to his influential "pre-occupation with beauty" as "the summum bonum" of existence.

INNES, CATHERINE L. "The Unity of Jean Toomer's *Cane*." *CLA Journal* 15 (March 1972): 306-22. A fine essay that discusses at some length the relation between Toomer's concept of literary unity and the ideas of Ouspensky and that attempts to demonstrate the unity of *Cane* by "concentrating on some of the recurring images and symbols in the book and tracing their relation to one another and to the theme and structure of the work as a whole."

KERMAN, CYNTHIA E. "Jean Toomer?—Enigma." *Indian Journal of American Studies* 7 (January 1977): 67-78. An informative discussion of similarities and differences between Toomer and other black Southern writers that stresses Toomer's enigmatic "singularity."

KRAFT, JAMES. "Jean Toomer's *Cane*." *Markam Review* 2 (October 1970): 61-63. Emphasizes Toomer's effort to dissolve conventional categories, to resolve tensions or conflicts, and to achieve unity in both art and life. Contains some interesting comments on symbolism and "kinetic" form in *Cane*.

KRASNEY, MICHAEL JAY. "Jean Toomer and the Quest for Consciousness." Diss. Univ. of Wisconsin, 1972. An analysis of the bulk of Toomer's canon. Krasney explores the reasons for Toomer's shift from "black artist to moral artist." To this end, Krasney examines extensively the material written after *Cane*.

LOCKE, ALAIN. "From *Native Son* to *Invisible Man:* A Review of the Literature of the Negro for 1952." *Phylon* 14 (First Quarter 1953): 34-44. Briefly comments on *Cane*'s originality, asserting that the novel represents the first of "three points of peak development in Negro fiction by Negro writers" in the author's reviewing experience.

MARGOLIES, EDWARD. *Native Sons: A Critical Study of Twentieth-Century Negro American Authors*. Philadelphia and New York: J. B. Lippincott, 1968. Discusses *Cane* in relation to the Harlem Renaissance and its supposed glorification of the Negro's primitive qualities, claiming that "in idealizing the 'primitivism' and the negritude of the Negro peasant, Toomer signaled the neoromantic attitudes of subsequent Negro authors in the twenties."

MARTIN, ODETTE C. "*Cane*: Method and Myth." *Obsidian* 2 (Spring 1976): 5-20. An excellent and wide-ranging analysis of *Cane* in terms of Toomer's own quest for "soul" and for "the lost promise of America." Especially valuable for its comments on the "collage" form of the novel on Toomer's use of biblical themes and references, and on his depiction of opposing principles—male versus female, white versus black—in American life.

MASON, CLIFFORD. "Jean Toomer's Black Authenticity." *Black World* 20 (November 1970): 70-76. Praises Toomer as a writer who "really talks to black people about themselves" and who faithfully represents "the triumph and the tragedy that existed hand-to-hand in black life."

MUNSON, GORHAM B. "The significance of Jean Toomer." *Opportunity* 3 (September 1925): 262-63. An important early assessment stressing Toomer's literary craftsmanship, his innovations in literary form and technique, and his quest for "personal wholeness" as an answer to the "veritable chaos" of the modern world. Praising Toomer's conviction "that in a disrupted age the first duty of the artist is to unify himself." Munson confidently predicts that Toomer's search for unity will lead to a "fusion of his experience...that will give profundity to his later work."

OXLEY, THOMAS L. G. "The Negro in World's Literature." *New York Amsterdam News*, March 28, 1928, p. 8. A biographical study of Toomer and an early, perceptive analysis of his talent. "Of life, not about life, he writes with an inexhaustible source of beauty and inspiration."

REILLY, JOHN M. "The Search for Black Redemption: Jean Toomer's *Cane*." *Studies in the Novel* 2(1970): 312-24. *Cane* is a quest book and remains essentially a search for identity. Reilly demonstrates that *Cane* contains some unifying elements and he proceeds to analyze certain portions of *Cane* in this context. "Today when the problem of its form no longer seems baffling, the relevance of *Cane* has, if anything, been increased, because its exploration of identity as a process of liberating the spontaneous self in an often oppressive environment we can see how *Cane* established the major terms of the twentieth century black writer's chief theme—the redemption of personality."

ROSENBLATT, ROGER. *Black Fiction*. Cambridge, Massachusetts: Harvard Univ. Press, 1974. Interprets *Cane* in terms of "a cyclical conception of black American history" according to which the black man "must to a certain extent be brutalized" in order to become "acceptable within a white framework." Gives special attention to "Box Seat" and "Kabnis."

ROSENFELD, PAUL. "Jean Toomer," *Men Seen*. New York: Dial Press, 1925, pp. 227-33. An early essay praising Toomer's talent and the merits of *Cane*. "Toomer's free gift has given him the vision of a parting soul, and lifted his voice in salutation to the folk-spirit of the negro South."

SCHULTZ, ELIZABETH. "Jean Toomer's 'Box Seat': The Possibility for 'Constructive Crises.'" *Black America Literature Forum* 13 (Spring 1979): 7-12. As a whole, *Cane* expresses Toomer's concern that racial division has splintered classes of people as well as individual operation. "Box Seat" is *Cane*'s "Most concise and dramatic expression of Toomer's yearning for the antagonists to be healed."

SOLARD, ALAIN. "The Impossible Unity: Jean Toomer's 'Kabnis'" In *Myth and Ideology in American Culture*. Ed. Regis Furand. Villeneuve-d'Ascq: Publications of the University of Lille III, 1976, pp. 175-94. A helpful attempt "to ascertain Toomer's own ideology within the American context of the Twenties." Solard discusses at length the ideological significance of various characters and events in "Kabnis" and comments on the ideological implications of Toomer's interest in achieving an integration of self and "a fusion of beings and races which would lift the curse that weighs upon them."

STEIN, MARIAN L. "The Poet-Observer and Fern in Jean Toomer's *Cane*." *Markham Review* 2 (October 1970): 64-65. An ingenious account of how Toomer's use of language subtly evokes "the special oneness and separateness of the poet-observer and Fern."

TURNER, DARWIN T. "The Failure of a Playwright." *CLA Journal* 10 (June 1967): A balanced, informative discussion of Toomer's plays. Turner stresses the innovative character of Toomer's experiments with "nonrepresentational technique and form" in drama and relates these experiments to such modern developments as Expressionism and Theater of the Absurd.

————. *In a Minor Chord: Three Afro-American Writers and Their Search for Identity*. Carbondale and Edwardsville, Illinois: Southern Illinois Univ. Press, 1971. Contains the most thorough and comprehensive account of Toomer's life, career, and works that has been published to date. Drawing upon a wealth of biographical and historical information, Turner carefully examines the various phases of the psychological, intellectual, and artistic development that led Toomer to spiritual "exile." In discussing individual works, Turner offers admirably balanced assessments of Toomer's strengths and limitations as a writer.

————. "Introduction." *Cane*, by Jean Toomer. New York: Liveright, 1975, pp. ix-xxv. An excellent introduction to Toomer's life, career, and works. Contains a brief but insightful analysis of *Cane* and much useful background information concerning the historical period in which this book was written.

_____. "Jean Toomer's *Cane*." *Negro Digest* 18 (January 1969): 59-64. A detailed and judicious analysis that emphasizes *Cane*'s weaknesses as well as its strengths, arguing that certain features of this work foreshadow the "death" of Toomer as a literary artist.

TURPIN, WATERS E. "Four Short Fiction Writers of the Harlem Renaissance—Their Legacy of Achievement," *CLA Journal* 11 (September 1967): 59-72. Discusses "Blood-Burning Moon," emphasizing Toomer's "skilled characterizations, his capturing of the atmosphere of a Southern milltown...and the poetry of his style."

VAN MOL, KAY R. "Primitivism and Intellect in Toomer's *Cane* and McKay's *Banana Bottom*: The Need for an Integrated Black Consciousness." *Negro American Literature Forum* 10 (Summer 1976): 48-52. A fine essay arguing that both novels "deal with the development of a black consciousness which is envisioned largely in terms of a reconciliation or blending of what might be called the 'intellect' of the Western world and the 'primitive' of the African heritage." Especially good on the ways in which male-female relationships in *Cane* exemplify the opposition between "intellect" and "primitivism."

WALDRON, EDWARD. "The Search for Identity in Jean Toomer's 'Esther.'" *CLA Journal* 14 (March 1971): 277-80. Discusses "Esther" as a story concerned with the following problematic relationships: the relationship between the American black and his African background and the relationship between the light-skinned American black and the American black community.

WATKINS, PATRICIA. "Is There a Unifying Theme in *Cane*?" *CLA Journal* 15 (March 1972): 303-305. Argues that the unifying theme of *Cane* is that of man's inability to communicate and interact with fellow humans; the inability to understand and therefore to love; the ability to quicken another human soul."

WESTERFIELD, HARGIS. "Jean Toomer's 'Fern': A Mythical Dimension." *CLA Journal* 14 (March 1971): 274-76. Explicates "the Jewish and Christian myth of the story," commenting on the meanings and functions of Toomer's biblical references.

WEYL, NATHANIEL. "New Mythology of the Negro Past." *National Review* 20 (October 8, 1968): 1020-22. A general comment and review of the present trend in Afro-Americn writing. *Cane* is mentioned as a work which contains such analyses and echoes.

WITHROW, DOLLY. "Cutting Through Shade." *CLA Journal* 21 (September 1977): 98-99. A detailed formal analysis of Toomer's "Reapers" that traces a progression from a message of "death and destruction" to a message of "hope."

Index